THE
FAMILY
INVESTOR

How Young Couples & Families Can Become
Wealthy

BY MICHAEL W ZISA

The Family Investor is dedicated to all couples and families striving to become financially responsible and financially educated. Also, a special thank you to the knowledgeable professionals who volunteered to share their thoughts. The Family Investor was written with inspiration from my wife, Kim, and my three sons Rob, Jack, and Kyle. I am, and always will be, a proud husband and father.

TABLE OF CONTENTS

—◆—

FORWARD

Young couples and families deal with many issues. From economic concerns to family planning and everything in between, life can seem overwhelming. Developing and maintaining a financial plan is an important step in preparing for the future. Financial planning is a strategy of meeting your life goals through careful management of your finances. It involves coordinating your financial background so that you can accomplish the following:

1. Analyze your current situation
2. Create goals for your future
3. Develop a long term investment plan
4. Keep attuned to your plan and make adjustments over time

Whatever your goals are for the future, now is the time to prepare for them. Your main ally is time! Though planning for goals down the road is important, today you need to look at your immediate financial needs.

Michael Zisa is passionately committed to helping young couples and families can begin and continue their quest for wealth. As a financial literacy and investing educator, Michael has inspired many high school students (including my daughter and son) to understand the importance of financial responsibility. Having visited Mike in his classroom, and witnessed his passion for teaching, this book can be a powerful first step in your future financial success. I believe that this book can help illustrate to young couples and families the critical need to become financially literate and responsible in today's complex society. Perhaps you are buying your first home, funding for your child's future college, wondering how to protect your family from financial hardships, or simply trying to figure out how to accumulate enough money to retire. This book can help guide you through the challenges that may be in your way or on the horizon.

I certainly wish that I understood basic financial concepts when my wife and I were starting out. Life is wonderfully chaotic, yet it is so important to stay focused through it all. And by that I mean financially focused. So open up this book and let the timeless and essential information help you create your personal financial plan.

Kent Elwell, Financial Professional

———

OUR BUSY, EXHAUSTING, & SOMETIMES OVERWHELMING LIVES

The alarm blasts its repetitive disturbance at 5:30 in the morning. After relentlessly attempting to press the snooze button, you struggle mightily to roll out of your warm, comfortable bed and start another day of sometimes imposing challenges involving your job, parenting, and your marriage. As you drag yourself into the hot shower, many redundant thoughts embrace your mind. You gloriously recall the first few years of matrimony, dreaming about how life was much different before the days of raising children and when your relationship with your spouse was much easier to keep fresh and exciting. These calming thoughts are *coincidentally* interrupted by the seemingly deafening sounds of unique cries from one of your children. You instinctively morph into parent mode and proceed to holler, over the serene sounds of the warm water rolling down your back, for your spouse to check on 'Junior'. "Maybe", you quickly think to yourself, "I can find a few minutes tonight to enjoy a few relaxing minutes at home". Unfortunately, you have to stay late at work today to work on a big project that needs to be completed by the end of the week. Hoping to advance your career, you know the project is extremely important and needs to be your first priority of your day.

It seems like you are always rushing to get ready for the day, always grabbing a small bite to eat, and saying a quick goodbye to your family. However, you understand that this is all for your loved ones and you would never let go.

Whether you are newly married, raising children, or recently divorced, financial responsibility should be an essential part of your life. Financial responsibility includes, but is not limited to, saving, investing, retirement planning, education planning, tax efficiency, debt management, and wealth protection. Most of us feel that these topics are boring or just too difficult to navigate through. However, being financial responsible is a necessity in today's complicated world of money management. Financial responsibility will make your life less stressful, empowers your family relationships, and can lead to a retirement lifestyle that you have always dreamed about.

As a financial literacy educator and financial advisor, I constantly preach to my students and clients about how their finances will get more complicated as time goes by. There are an endless number of rules, theories, forms, and methodologies that are out there that seem to only complicate your financial lives. The purpose of 'The Family Investor' is to educate you, in a simplified manner, on how to sift through the financial maze and have a resource of key financial concepts. I will teach you the importance of an emergency fund and developing a budget, how to manage debt responsibly, save for your children's college expenses, minimize your taxes, invest for the future, how to protect your wealth, and much more. The most important thing is that you have taken the initiative to read this book and should be commended for taking the first step. You may feel overwhelmed at times with all of the valuable information you will receive, but isn't your significant other and your family worth it?

You will find that over time you will be farther ahead than most other couples and families from a financial perspective.

I'd like to mention one more thing before we begin Chapter 1. One of the most important aspects of thriving financially is to live within your means. That is, do not buy things you cannot afford!! I realize that I am stating the obvious, but many of us spend, spend, and then spend some more even though we do not have the money to pay for it. This is a recipe for disaster. I find it amazing that, throughout my lifetime, it seems as though our society has elevated what it means to be successful and happy. No longer can we be satisfied with a smaller home, a basic cell phone, a weekend vacation to the local mountains with the family, or even a simplistic, reliable car. Absolutely not!! We convince ourselves we *need* a much bigger home, the latest and greatest smartphone, a week or more all-inclusive vacation on a tropical island, and a much fancier car that our friends will admire. There is certainly nothing wrong with wanting a better life for you and your family, and if you can afford to pay for these things, there is nothing wrong with buying them. However, most of us do not fall into that category, especially if you have a young family. Consequently, many people who have high incomes tend to proportionally spend their money in relation to what they make in salary. Therefore, are most people really getting ahead financially?

Happiness is the true key to success for ourselves and for our families. Money does help, but does not define true happiness. True happiness can be found within yourself and with your loved ones. I sometimes have discussions with people about how I can be very happy if I didn't have all of the superficial "stuff" that occupies my life. I just *need* my family, friends, and my health (and maybe an 80-inch big screen TV!!☺). And as much as I love our home, it does not define my happiness. I could be just as happy renting an apartment! I realize that may sound ridiculous to some people, but it is the truth. I truly believe that all of us need to take a step back and do some soul-searching to rediscover the simple things in life. I am confident that you will see that the simple things are the ones that make us who we are. These can include activities such as spending time talking with your friends and family (actually talking....NOT always through social media), going on a family hike, having a family game night, exercising with your significant other, and even religious activities. Any of these activities can be self-fulfilling and, of course, are much less expensive than many of the frivolous things we tend to frequently buy. And remember, your true friends will not judge you based on the type of car you drive or how much money you make. True friends will appreciate you because you are a good, kind, humble, and giving person.

Now that all of the sentimental moments of the book are finished, it's time to get to work! I'm sure you are excited about the upcoming chapters in 'The Family Investor' and I am certain that the information you receive will be an asset to you and your family for years to come. Let's get started!

CHAPTER ONE

———

ESTABLISHING GOALS, A BUDGET, AND AN EMERGENCY FUND

Jim's career is thriving and has generated a sizable yearly income for him and his family throughout his work years. He easily makes over $100,000 per year not including his annual bonus. Jim and his wife, Mary, live in a modest home and have two children. They are both 50 years old now and would like to retire by the time they reach 60. However, Jim and Mary have always been spenders. To make matters worse, they have absolutely no idea where their money goes. They also do not have a good grasp on how much money is coming in. Consequently, they have a negative net worth. What does a negative net worth mean you might ask? Quite simply, if Jim and Mary sold all of their assets (things they own), they would not have enough cash to pay off their liabilities (money they owe). I hope you can foresee that it is highly unlikely that Jim and Mary will be able to retire at 60. Furthermore, Jim will likely be working for many years after his 60th birthday. How is this possible? Well, never in their lives have they developed a spending plan, also known as a *budget*. A budget is simply an estimate of expected income and expenses for a given period in the future, usually monthly. *Budgeting* is an easy technique where you estimate your income and expenses. By doing this, you can monitor how much money you are spending on certain items and services. Basically, you need to know where your money is going. You need to know how much money is coming in and how much money is going out. This is also called *cash flow*. If more money is going out than coming in, you have negative cash flow. If more money is coming in than going out, you have positive cash flow.

An important aspect of a budget is to set aside money each month to build a cash reserve, also known as an *emergency fund*. An emergency fund is money you have set aside for the purpose of providing income for your family in case of a significant event in your life. For example, you may lose your job and be out of work for a specific time period. Or maybe one of your extended family members becomes seriously ill and they need help paying their medical expenses. Maybe you unexpectedly are in dire need of a new roof on your home. Whatever the case may be, something always seems to happen at some point in your life that will negatively affect your financial situation. Ideally, you should have an emergency fund equal to 3-6 months of living expenses, preferably 6 months.

The money you have built up in an emergency fund should be kept in short-term instruments such as certificate of deposits (CDs) or money market accounts. Another alternative is to simply hold the money in a savings account. Either way, the money needs to be easily accessible and very safe. **Building an emergency fund and developing a budget is the foundation of every financial plan!**

Another important aspect of a budget is to establish financial goals. In general, there are two types of financial goals:

- **Short term**- These are goals that you want to attain in approximately 1-5 years. Some examples of short-term goals are:

   o   Buying a car
   o   Saving $1,000
   o   Going on a family vacation
   o   Buying a home

- **Long term**- These are goals that you want to attain in approximately 6 or more years. Some examples of long-term goals are:
   o   Saving for retirement
   o   Saving for college expenses for your children
   o   Buying a vacation home

Everyone has different goals. However, there are some general guidelines on how to establish short-term and long-term goals. First of all, your goals should be S.M.A.R.T. Let's take a look at how this acronym can help us:

Specific:	Your goals should be clearly defined and described in detail
Measurable:	You should be able to track your progress toward a definite endpoint
Attainable:	Your goals should be realistic and reachable
Relevant:	Your goals should be relevant to *your* specific needs and values
Timely:	Your goals should be subject to a clear deadline

Next, there are specific steps you should take when establishing your goals:

1. List your goals
2. Divide up your goals according to how long it will take to meet each goal

3. Estimate the cost of each goal
4. Calculate how much you need to set aside each period
5. Prioritize your goals
6. Create a schedule for meeting your goals

DEVELOPING A BUDGET (SPENDING PLAN)

When creating your budget, there are some obvious income sources and expenses you need to track. Some examples of income sources are your salary, bonuses, interest from a bank account, a tax refund, and earnings from your investments, which we will discuss in detail later in the book. Expenses usually fall into two spending categories; discretionary and nondiscretionary. *Discretionary spending* is money you spend on products and services that are generally unnecessary such as eating out or a lavish vacation. I am definitely guilty of spending too much money on eating out. Yes, it is convenient, and it is certainly enjoyable. However, my family could save quite a bit of money if we simply cooked our own meals most of the time.

Non-discretionary spending is money you spend on essential items that you need to live such as your rent or mortgage payment, utilities, clothes, transportation expenses, and groceries. Of course, there are different levels of how much you need to spend on these necessary items. Buying a very large home is probably not in your best financial interest since a huge home comes with larger expenses. When succumbing to a large home, you can expect to have a much higher monthly mortgage payment, higher property taxes, higher property insurance costs, and higher utilities expenses. And don't forget about the money you will need to spend on the extra furniture needed to fill up all of those large rooms! In other words, you do not want your home to become your money pit. Many owners of big homes find themselves living paycheck to paycheck because of the high costs associated with them. If the owner loses his or her job, they run the risk of losing their home in foreclosure. This is a situation you want to avoid at all costs (no pun intended!). The same issue applies when buying an expensive car. Yes, it is wonderful to have that beefed up SUV or even a glamorous BMW or Lexus. However, with an expensive car comes higher ongoing costs. Not only will your car payment be higher, but your auto insurance will likely be higher. Furthermore, a car is a *depreciating asset*. A depreciating asset is something you own that goes down in value over time. Also, an expensive car usually means higher maintenance costs. For example, it is much more costly to replace the tires and other items on an SUV when compared to a minivan. As a matter of fact, repairs on SUVs can cost a great deal more when compared to a minivan or even most sedans. I am often amused at many people I meet who refuse to ever buy a minivan. I never really understood why, except that maybe they do not want to be perceived as the stereotypical soccer Mom or a label similar to that. Quite honestly, we bought a minivan when my second son was born and I can say, without regret, that it was one of our smartest purchases, especially after we had our third son!

I'd like to disclose that my intention is not to diminish anyone's decision to buy a big home or fancy car. Each of us has our own priorities and some of us are able to afford these items without breaking their bank account. My goal is to help you make smarter decisions for you and your family so that you can maintain a happy and healthy financial lifestyle that will not cause you pain and suffering along the way. Remember to take a step back when making large purchases and ask yourself if you really need it. A large home or a fancy car will NOT make you happier. Maybe it will temporarily make you happy, but like every other material item, the happiness effect will weaken over time.

While I mentioned some expenses above, there are many expense items that are not as obvious. These can be items or services such as charitable donations, a gym membership, entertainment costs, life insurance premiums, pet expenses, and more. It is important to account for every type of expense in your budget. Table 1.1 on the following page illustrates a typical list of many expenses that could be in your budget. However, many of us will have different expense items listed due to our unique lifestyles. Either way, one of the golden rules of estimating expenses is to be CONSERVATIVE! In other words, estimate your expenses on the high side because you never want to be caught short. Keep in mind, you can always reduce the amount you have in your budget for certain expenses if you find that your actual expenses are far below what you expected.

When it comes to budgeting, the golden rule to live by is to **PAY YOURSELF FIRST!** That is, always take an adequate amount of money from every paycheck and either save or invest it. Whatever you have left should be used for your expenses. If you find that there is not enough money left to cover your expenses, you may need to change your lifestyle. Keep in mind that the amount you should save or invest from your paycheck will be different for each of us. However, the trick is to have the amount you save dictate the amount of money you have left for your expenses.

One huge advantage of a budget is to determine where you can cut costs. For example, you may have $500 per month set aside for family entertainment costs. However, you realize that you could probably reduce that to $400 per month after realizing that you do not spend $500 per month on family entertainment. Now you just found an additional $100 per month to save and invest! As a matter of fact, the BEST way to increase your cash flow is to reduce your expenses. In the words of one of my clients who was unemployed for almost a full year, "It's amazing how much money you can save by reducing your expenses when you have your back against the wall". Although my client was in a much different situation than most of us, it still is important to understand that reducing expenses is a vital part of prospering financially.

Table 1.1

EXPENSES
MORTGAGE OR RENT PAYMENT
CLOTHING
DENTAL
EYE CARE/CONTACTS
CO-PAYS/PRESCRIPTIONS
HAIRCUTS
GROCERIES
HOLIDAY GIFTS
BIRTHDAY GIFTS
HEALTH/DENTAL INSURANCE
AUTO INSURANCE
LIFE INSURANCE
DRY CLEANING
BOOKS/MAGAZINES
GYM MEMBERSHIP
DINING OUT
PARTIES/EVENTS
HOUSEHOLD PRODUCTS & REPAIRS
INTERNET/CABLE/PHONE
UTILITIES
VACATION EXPENSES
GASOLINE
CAR MAINTENANCE/REPAIRS
GASOLINE
CAR PAYMENT

Other ways to increase your cash flow include:

- Increase your income (get another job!!)
- Sell some of your assets
- Adjust your withholding on your paycheck to increase your net (take-home) pay

Acquiring a second job is a viable solution for many families who would like to increase their cash flow. It is understandably easier for younger couples with no children to work multiple jobs, but families with children can certainly do so if needed. Furthermore, at the risk of sounding abrasive, it is not beneath anyone's dignity to have another job, even if it requires manual labor. Older generations have another word for this--opportunity!! Prior to my wife and I having children, I had multiple jobs including teaching night school in a dangerous part of New York City, tutoring some evenings after my full-time job, and bartending on weekends. I was also taking classes towards my graduate degree at the time. Essentially, the point I am trying to make is that you have to do what you need to do sometimes to get ahead financially. Consequently, the additional income from my other jobs helped my wife and I save for a down payment on our first home, which would have been difficult to accumulate otherwise. Quite possibly, the additional income many people would receive from a second job could be used for other financially beneficial items such as a college savings plan, a retirement account, or an investment account. We will discuss these in detail in the forthcoming chapters.

How many of us have "stuff" taking over valuable space in our homes? It's astonishing walking around my house some days gazing at all of the things we own that occupy every nook and cranny of every room. And that is not even mentioning everything we have stored away (or shall I say piled high) in closets and the attic! I am going to try to put a positive spin on this dilemma--convert some of these assets into cash! It is easier than you may think. You can simply have a garage sale, place local ads on websites such as Craigslist, or even list many of these items on ebay. My wife does a wonderful job generating additional income for our family by using some of these methods. It also simplifies our life by getting rid of the clutter that invaded our home. Although you will not become wealthy by selling your "stuff" from time to time, it is another positive way to increase your cash flow. You never know.....maybe you will generate enough cash to go on a nice vacation!

The third bullet point involves reducing the amount of taxes that are automatically taken out of your paychecks. The way to make this happen is to fill out a W-4 form and claim additional exemptions. Your payroll department usually has W-4 forms available to you for your convenience. Be careful, however, because you want to make sure you are having enough money taken out to cover your income taxes for the year. In other words, you do not want to owe Uncle Sam money when you file your tax return. It can be tricky figuring out how many exemptions to claim on your W-4 without having a tax liability at the end of the year. However, if you have found that you usually get back a few thousand dollars in a tax refund from Uncle Sam, you definitely want to consider increasing your exemptions. I realize some people enjoy getting that large refund every year, but why would you want the government to hold some of your hard-earned dollars for so long? I suppose if you are not disciplined enough to use the money in a responsible way, it may be a good idea to get that big refund check every year. However, the purpose of reading 'The Family Investor' is to develop yourself into a financially responsible and disciplined person.

There are many tools and templates that are available for constructing a budget. Microsoft and Google have budget spreadsheets available that you can download for free. Additionally, there are many software programs and websites that you can use to create and maintain a budget. A good example of this is Quicken, which many computers have pre-installed. If you are comfortable maintaining your budget online, budgettracker.com and Mint.com are reputable websites to consider. Google also has an online app available called Goodbudget. These resources can sometimes be challenging to learn, but are well worth your time.

Key Points to Remember from Chapter 1

- Accumulate an emergency fund equal to 3-6 months of your monthly expenses.
- Create a prioritized list of your short and long-term financial goals.
- Develop and maintain a monthly spending plan (budget) every year.
- Be conservative when estimating your expenses.
- Analyze where you can reduce your expenses to increase your cash flow.
- Pay yourself first!

CHAPTER TWO

——◆——

THE GOLDEN RULE: STAY OUT OF DEBT!!

Your good friends Rick and Janet Jones have an amazingly similar family structure when compared to your family. Like you and your spouse, they have two boys ages 10 and 8 along with a 4 year old daughter. Their children attend the same school district as yours. They own a home about the same size as yours. As a matter of fact, there are numerous similarities between the two families.

One evening Rick and Janet invite your family out to dinner. They suggest going to a fancy steakhouse which can turn out to be quite an expensive choice for the typical family. Hesitantly, you and your spouse accept the invitation and wind up charging almost $500 on your credit card that night. The following week Rick and Janet invite you out again for a lavish dinner at the nearby casino along with some friendly gambling afterwards. This time you politely decline because you understand that you should not keep charging these needless expenses to your credit card. You understand that your family's needs are much more important than keeping up with the Joneses (literally!!).

A few months go by and Rick pulls into your driveway in a brand new, shiny, Mercedes Benz including a sunroof, a premium sound system, the best navigation system money can buy, and all the added bells and whistles that most people never use. Your first thought to yourself is why the heck does he need a new car, especially since his other one was just three years old and only had 20,000 miles on it. As you try to rationalize this in your head, Rick jumps out with unmatched enthusiasm and a grin as wide as a football field. As he begins to gloat about his expensive new depreciating asset, you glance over at your dependable, and paid for, five-year-old sedan and think to yourself about how that is all you need right now. Once again, you understand that there are more important things to worry about right now than being seen in a glamorous new car. Furthermore, you are very happy that you fully *own* your car and have no monthly payments to make.

Another few months go by and Rick invites your family over for a weekend barbeque. Upon entering their backyard, you notice the brand new, top of the line outdoor furniture along with a fancy new oversized grill, and exquisite stone pavers that line the new deck area. Now you are thinking that Rick must have earned a huge promotion from his company and is making a significant amount of money. However, something seems a little different at the Jones household this time around. Rick appears to be a little stressed out and is not his usual laid back and always-smiling self. Also, it is apparent that there is tension between Rick and Janet and they are trying to disguise it without much success. After finishing your meal, you and your family decide to leave because you feel like you are interrupting a potential argument between Rick and Janet. You arrive home and glance at your backyard with all of your modest, but fully functional, furnishings.

Five years later, after Rick & Janet moved into a brand new ginormous (is that a word?!) home in a gated and impeccably landscaped neighborhood, you see Rick at the local grocery store. He looks worn down, out of shape, and unhappy. He proceeds to confess to you that he and Janet recently went through a bitter divorce. He practically begs you to come back to his lonely home to catch up on old times and to discuss his situation. After reluctantly agreeing, you follow him home and are enthralled by the massive homes that line the streets of his neighborhood and provide a background for the championship golf course, Olympic-size pool, and luxurious clubhouse.

After several hours of depressing conversation with Rick, you head home and discuss his timeline of life events with your spouse. Not surprisingly, Rick's past events include:

- Maxing out his credit card to buy numerous discretionary and needless items
- Opening up a 2nd credit card and maxing out that card as well (on *more* frivolous items)
- Taking a huge loan out to buy his wonderful new Mercedes-Benz (a depreciating asset)
- Obtaining an incredibly large mortgage to buy his gigantic home (what some people might call a 'McMansion')
- Having difficulty keeping up with the monthly mortgage payments
- Losing sleep most nights worrying about how much debt he has piled up
- Constantly fighting with his wife (before the divorce) about their lack of savings and their pitiful net worth
- Seeing his children negatively affected by the constant tension in his home
- Losing half of his assets in the divorce
- Losing full custody of his children
- Realizing that he must sell his large dwelling and likely lose money on the sale given his large outstanding loan balance

- Having issues getting work completed at his job due to the above circumstances

This scenario may seem extreme to some people. However, one of the biggest reasons why marriages end is due to money, or the lack thereof. This is obviously not an optimal way for your family to live. Too many times in our society we try to keep up with the Joneses. We buy bigger houses, really cool cars, fancy gadgets, and useless junk to make ourselves 'happy' and to hope people *perceive* us as successful and wealthy. Hopefully, you can admit to yourself that using debt in an irresponsible way can cause financial disaster and can be detrimental to your loved ones. In this chapter we will learn about the different types of debt available to you and which ones to avoid completely.

THE EVIL CREDIT CARD

Credit cards can be an important component of your ongoing finances. However, credit cards can also be the demise of your financial well-being. Many adults have used credit cards to purchase unnecessary and frivolous items only to put themselves in severe debt that can prove to be inescapable. When using a credit card, it is important to remember that you are borrowing money that you have to pay back. If you are disciplined enough to use it responsibly you can establish good credit. Establishing good credit can help you get approved for other types of loans (such as a car or home loan) and will allow you to be offered a lower interest rate from the lender.

It is so empowering to possess a credit card knowing that you can go out and just buy things by using that gorgeous little rectangle piece of plastic. Most people are already well aware of the risks when using credit cards. But what *really* is a credit card and how can it affect your financial life, positively or negatively? And why do many of us insist on using them in an irresponsible way? The reason is that, as previously mentioned, we live in a society that influences us to have the best of everything, whenever we want. We feel it is 'necessary' to buy, buy, and buy some more so that we can enjoy the good life and be happier. Our family, friends, and neighbors need to perceive us as successful. What better way to do that then to *look* like we are wealthy?! And that is a big part of the problem. To live this kind of lifestyle, most of us need to buy things on credit because we do not have the cash to pay for it right away. Many times this leads us to fall into a vicious cycle of constant debt that seems to snowball out of control faster than the most expensive Lamborghini.

There are two types of credit card users:

1. Revolvers
2. Transactors

A *revolver* is the term banks and credit card companies use for people who do NOT pay their entire balance off by the monthly due date. For example, if you bought $1,000 worth of products one month, but only pay the minimum payment by the due date, you will be charged a very high interest rate on your unpaid balance. In many cases, interest rates can be as high as 25-30%!! It is practically impossible to become wealthy when you are paying high interest rates on your credit card. Credit card companies LOVE revolvers. **Don't be a revolver!!**

Conversely, a *transactor* is the term banks and credit card companies use for people who always pay off the *full* monthly balance by the due date. Transactors are highly disciplined and never pay interest to the banks because they do not have any unpaid balances from month to month. As long as you remain a transactor, you can take advantage of a rewards credit card and generate points that you can use to buy a variety of products. Some rewards cards allow you to use your points for cash or even airline tickets!! Banks and credit card companies dislike transactors. **ALWAYS be a transactor!!**

As a former financial analyst in the credit department at a large bank, it is astonishing to me how much information financial institutions have about us. They use this information to target people who are revolvers or are most likely to become revolvers. This is big business for these institutions who reap huge profits from their credit card divisions. Please keep this in mind the next time you receive any credit card offer in the mail or online. Read the fine print!! Understand the terms of the offer. Every credit card offer is required to display the terms of the credit card agreement in what is known as a *Schumer's Box*. Furthermore, do not fall for many of their marketing schemes including 'teaser rates' and 'balance transfer offers'. Teaser rates are offered to entice you to apply for a credit card. Many times they will advertise a teaser rate of 0% on all purchases for a specific time period. Wow! Zero percent! It sounds like such a fantastic deal that many of us will use that credit card unwisely because we think we can afford to buy more since we are not paying any interest. However, the fine print (or shall I say the barely readable tiny text) will detail what happens if you do not pay off your balance by the end of the teaser rate period. For example, let's say that you charged about $3,000 on your awesome credit card with a zero percent teaser rate for the first three months. By the time the fourth month rolls around, you only paid off $1,000 of your $3,000 balance. Well, you will be happy (or unhappy) to know that your *friendly* credit card company will now charge you an astronomical interest rate on your unpaid balance. Additionally, many credit card companies will make you pay the accrued interest that you acquired in the first three months because you did not pay it off before the teaser rate expired. In other words, your unpaid balance now carries interest charges just as though you NEVER had a zero percent interest rate on your purchases during the first few months. Isn't that super nice of them?! You can tell they really care about you! (Can you sense the sarcasm?)

Balance transfer offers are another way credit card companies try to 'earn' your business. Many balance transfer offers seem like an amazing deal on the surface, but only serve as a facade. Their goal is to lure you in so you transfer all of your unpaid balances from another credit card, or even multiple cards, by offering you terms you can't refuse. Their calculated hope is that you will become a revolver and make them lots of money in the future. However, the biggest risk with balance transfers is that many people will use them to delay the inevitable. They will continue to transfer their unpaid balances from card to card knowing that they are taking advantage of the usual 0% interest rate for the first few months. This will result in a lower credit score due to all of the cards they are opening. Also, it will eventually lead to either missing a payment or piling up more debt during the entire process of transferring the balances. Once again, this is a vicious cycle that is extremely difficult to unwind.

A famous billionaire once mentioned that even he can't make money through investing if he holds credit card debt. For example, if the average annual return on a $5,000 investment is 8% and the interest rate on $5,000 in unpaid balances from a credit card is 15%, it is highly unlikely you will ever make money. In fact, you are *very* likely to lose money unless you get lucky from your $5,000 investment and earn more than 15% on it every year. Keep in mind that the average annual return in the stock market, historically speaking, is approximately 10%. However, when it comes to investing, you should not have *all* of your money in stocks. Hence, the 8% average return we are using in the example. Obviously, it would be extremely difficult to make money when owning credit card debt. That is why you should never invest your money without paying off your unpaid credit card balances first. The following are examples of using a credit card responsibly:

- You walk into an electronics store and see a super cool HDTV that you really want. It costs $1,000, but you only have $300 saved to pay for it. Instead of using your credit card, you decide to wait until you have enough saved up to allow you to pay off the entire balance by the due date.
- You recently received your first credit card with a credit limit of $500. After using your card to pay a necessary $500 car repair bill, you are smart enough to realize you cannot use your card again until you make a payment. (If you do use it before making a payment, you will exceed your credit limit and be charged significant fees)
- You receive numerous credit card balance transfer offers and introductory rates in the mail. You proceed to put them through the shredder!

Believe it or not, there are some advantages to owning a credit card. The greatest advantage, as previously mentioned, is that you can establish good credit by using your card responsibly. By "responsibly", I mean that you only purchase things that you need and you have the money available to pay your ENTIRE credit card balance off by the due date. Other advantages include:

- **Convenience**. Having a credit card is good when you do not have much cash in your pocket.
- **Organized record**. Your credit card statement lists all of your purchases allowing you to keep a record of everything you purchased.
- **Rewards**. Some credit cards offer reward points for making purchases.

- **Purchase protection**. Credit card companies will usually offer a line of protection against fraudulent activities on your card or any disputes with merchants.

It is important to note that a rewards card can lead to excessive purchases if not used in a disciplined manner. Yes, it is fantastic to earn points and redeem them for gift cards, electronic items, and even airline tickets. However, some consumers will overspend just to accumulate more points. This path will definitely lead to becoming a revolver at some point.

My wife and I have a rewards card that we have had for many years. We actually charge as many of our expenses to the card as possible. We can do this because we always have the money to pay off the balance every month. We have NEVER paid the credit card company any interest! They do not like us because we are revolvers. We legally play the 'system' and actually *make* money by using our card. We usually redeem our rewards points for gift cards from clothing stores. Therefore, our clothing expenses can be reduced in our budget. Furthermore, we have increased our cash flow which means that we will have additional funds to save or invest.

I'd like to discuss what to do if you are a revolver and have a significant unpaid balance. The following real-life application will help you make smart decisions when putting together a strategy to pay off your existing credit card debt:

Ed has been financially irresponsible lately, evidenced by the many frivolous items he has bought with his credit card over the last year. He now finds himself with two credit cards and has a balance of $3,000 on each of them. One card has an interest rate of 18% while the other charges a rate of 25%. Ed now realizes he needs to quickly change his habits before he digs himself into a financial hole *that will be extremely difficult to climb out. Although Ed has been spending much of his money, he still is investing about $300 per month. Consider the following questions:*

1. *Which card should Ed pay off first?*
2. *Should Ed continue to invest $300 month while he is paying off his credit card balances?*

Although both credit cards have high interest rates, Ed should obviously pay off the credit card that charges a higher one--25%. Once he pays off that balance, he should then focus his attention on paying off the balance on the other card. Ed should also stop investing $300 per month until his credit card balances are completely paid off. It is very difficult to make more than 18-25% on your investments in one year without taking on too much risk. Ed needs to put his priorities into perspective and attain balance in his life.

Another way that Ed could help himself is by consolidating his credit card debt by taking out a loan from a bank to pay off his balances. The interest rate on the loan will likely be much lower than the rates on the credit cards. As always, Ed needs to be disciplined by making sure he will not be irresponsible again by making unnecessary purchases and accumulating unpaid balances.

<u>Things to Do When Using a Credit Card</u>

- Do pay off your balance by the due date--be a transactor!!
- Do find a 'no annual fee' card
- Do review your credit card statement each month
- Do use your card responsibly
- Do stay within your credit limit

<u>Things You *Don't* Do When Using a Credit Card</u>

- Don't be a revolver!!
- Don't use your card if you do not have the money to pay off the entire balance by the due date
- Don't get multiple credit cards
- Don't get fooled into a card with introductory rates
- Don't get in the habit of taking balance transfer offers
- Don't take cash advances from your credit card

BEWARE OF 'NO INTEREST/NO PAYMENTS' ADVERTISING

One evening, while watching television with your family, you come across a fabulous commercial that seems too good to be true. The commercial states that you can purchase all the new furniture you need and not pay a single penny of interest or monthly payments for three years! Additionally, you are not required to make a down payment on your purchase (this is called a "No Money Down" offer). Giddy with this once-in-a-lifetime 'opportunity', you take your family on a trip to the furniture store to check out a new couch and matching chairs and coffee table for your entertainment room. While you're there, the salesman talks you into buying more furniture for your living room because of the super special they have going on that he says will only last until the end of the day. What an unbelievably great day you are having! You can purchase tons of furniture at a heavily discounted price (according to your friendly neighborhood furniture salesman) and not have to pay for three years!! A couple of hours later you finally leave the store and are anxious for your new furniture selections you bought for around $5,000 to be delivered to your home (with "free" delivery).

Over the next few years, the excitement of the new furniture has abated. With your busy calendar, you completely forget that you have to begin paying for all of it at the end of the 3-year period. Suddenly, you receive a notification from the store explaining that you need to either pay for all of the furniture at once or begin making monthly payments. The letter explains in the fine print that all of the interest that you supposedly didn't have to pay has accrued over the last few years. You only buy the furniture interest free if you pay for everything in full by the end of the three years.

"How could this have happened?" you ask yourself as if you are crying out for someone to rescue you from this financial nightmare. You realize that you cannot afford to pay the entire $5,000 by the due date because you did not set aside the money for it over the previous 36 months. Reluctantly, you begin making the monthly payments while paying close to 25% in interest on your unpaid balance, not to mention all of the interest that has accrued. Unfortunately, that super $5,000 deal has become much costlier and will be a thorn in your budget as well as your financial plan until you figure out how to pay for it sooner.

My family and I succumbed to this situation many years ago, and although we did pay for everything in full by the due date, I always had it hanging over my head causing me stress and anxiety. I fully understand that I did not have to pay any interest or make payments along the way, but was it really worth it? For some people it might be and that is fine. However, many people will fall into the trap and wind up paying much more for things because they do not have the discipline to save the money in a short amount of time. The stores that promote these 'super deals' do not want you to pay in full by the due date. They want you to pay the astronomical interest rates so they can make a boatload of money. They are certainly not trying to be nice. They are in business to make money.

It is very important to stay away from these potentially disastrous situations to maintain a healthy financial lifestyle. If it sounds too good to be true, it usually is not a good deal. When faced with these circumstances, please remember to take a step back and really think about the decision you are making. Generally speaking, if you do not have the money to pay for it, don't buy it. Period.

Key Points to Remember from Chapter 2

- Always live debt free
- Don't be a revolver
- Always be a transactor

CHAPTER THREE

HOME OWNERSHIP & MANAGING YOUR MORTGAGE

So you want to own a home? Or maybe you already own a home. Most of us do not have enough cash to simply pay for the full price of a house. Consequently, we need to take out a loan to allow us into the wonderful world of home ownership. I use the word 'wonderful' with a bit of sarcasm because owning a home can be a valuable asset, but comes with a huge amount of responsibility. Anyway, in the case of home ownership, taking out a mortgage is necessary for most of us. In this section, I will explain the various types of loans available to you when purchasing your largest asset. I will also detail the differences between a home equity loan and a home equity line of credit and how you can drastically reduce the amount of interest you pay over the life of the loan.

There are a few concepts to discuss before moving forward. The first concept is called *equity*. Equity, in the context of home ownership, is the amount of cash you have in your home. In other words, it is the difference between what your home is worth and the amount you owe on your mortgage. For example, if your home is valued at $300,000 and you owe $220,000 on your mortgage, you have $80,000 of equity. Another way to look at it is if you actually sold your home for $300,000 and paid off your $220,000 mortgage.

In that case you would walk away with $80,000 in cash. Of course you have to understand that I am not deducting any commissions for the real estate agent or other potential fees, but I think you get the idea.

If you have never owned a home, you should understand that most banks will require a 20% *down payment*. A down payment is the amount of cash you need as an initial payment to purchase a home before the bank will consider lending you the remaining amount. For example, if you buy a home for $320,000, the bank will expect you to pay $64,000 in cash ($320,000 x 20%) before they would lend you the remaining $256,000 ($320,000 - $64,000). Some lenders only require 10% or lower, while a few might offer you a down payment of 0%. **STAY AWAY** from these offers!! You need to look no further than what happened in 2008-2009 with the real estate bubble and predatory lending (along with other shady investments) that sent the entire United States economy into a severe recession.

CHOOSING AND MANAGING AN APPROPRIATE HOME MORTGAGE

There are numerous types of mortgages you can use to finance a home. However, some of them are extremely risky and are not going to be discussed in the 'Family Investor'. These risky loans are 'too good to be true' and can cause you financial hardship. Stay away from offers such as interest-only loans, balloon mortgages, and reverse mortgages. As a financial advisor, I am unable to even offer clients reverse mortgages for good reason. The following list of mortgages can be appropriate for people depending on their goals, financial situation, and risk tolerance:

1. 30-year fixed mortgage (also known as a 'conventional' mortgage)
2. 15-year fixed mortgage
3. Adjustable-rate mortgages (ARMs)

A 30-year fixed mortgage is the most popular home loan among homeowners. Some advantages of a 30-year fixed mortgage include:

- Offers the chance to borrow money on a long-term basis, without having to worry about a change in interest rates or payments
- Monthly payments are lower when compared to a 15-year fixed mortgage
- Lower monthly payments free up money that borrowers can put into investments
- Higher interest bill increases the amount you can deduct at tax time (if your total itemized deductions exceeds the standard deduction)

Disadvantages of a 30-year fixed mortgage include:

- Borrowers build equity at a slow rate
- The overall amount you pay in interest is much larger than other loans
- Interest rates are usually higher than those on a 15-year loan

One of the main reasons why so many people choose a 30-year fixed loan is that it allows them to be able to afford to buy a home in the first place. A 30-year mortgage, as opposed to a 15-year mortgage, allows the monthly payments to remain within the budgets of most people. Conversely, a 30-year mortgage builds equity much slower because most of your monthly payment in the early years of the loan goes to the bank in the form of interest. That means that a very small portion of the payment actually goes to reducing the

Table 3.1

Year	Balance	Payment	Principal	Interest	Equity	Total Interest	Total Payments
1	$197,300.83	$1,073.64	$251.56	$822.09	$2,950.73	$9,932.99	$12,883.72
2	$194,212.00	$1,073.64	$264.43	$809.22	$6,052.43	$19,715.01	$25,767.44
3	$190,965.14	$1,073.64	$277.96	$795.69	$9,312.81	$29,338.35	$38,651.16
4	$187,552.17	$1,073.64	$292.18	$781.47	$12,740.00	$38,794.87	$51,534.88
5	$183,964.59	$1,073.64	$307.12	$766.52	$16,342.54	$48,076.06	$64,418.59
6	$180,193.46	$1,073.64	$322.84	$750.81	$20,129.38	$57,172.93	$77,302.31
7	$176,229.38	$1,073.64	$339.35	$734.29	$24,109.97	$66,076.06	$90,186.03
8	$172,062.50	$1,073.64	$356.72	$716.93	$28,294.21	$74,775.54	$103,069.75
9	$167,682.44	$1,073.64	$374.97	$698.68	$32,692.53	$83,260.94	$115,953.47
10	$163,078.28	$1,073.64	$394.15	$679.49	$37,315.87	$91,521.32	$128,837.19
11	$158,238.56	$1,073.64	$414.32	$659.33	$42,175.75	$99,545.16	$141,720.91
12	$153,151.24	$1,073.64	$435.51	$638.13	$47,284.27	$107,320.35	$154,604.63
13	$147,803.64	$1,073.64	$457.79	$615.85	$52,654.16	$114,834.19	$167,488.35
14	$142,182.44	$1,073.64	$481.22	$592.43	$58,298.78	$122,073.29	$180,372.07
15	$136,273.65	$1,073.64	$505.84	$567.81	$64,232.18	$129,023.60	$193,255.78
16	$130,062.56	$1,073.64	$531.72	$541.93	$70,469.15	$135,670.35	$206,139.50
17	$123,533.70	$1,073.64	$558.92	$514.72	$77,025.22	$141,998.00	$219,023.22
18	$116,670.81	$1,073.64	$587.51	$486.13	$83,916.71	$147,990.23	$231,906.94
19	$109,456.80	$1,073.64	$617.57	$456.07	$91,160.78	$153,629.88	$244,790.66
20	$101,873.70	$1,073.64	$649.17	$424.47	$98,775.46	$158,898.91	$257,674.38
21	$93,902.65	$1,073.64	$682.38	$391.26	$106,779.74	$163,778.36	$270,558.10
22	$85,523.77	$1,073.64	$717.29	$356.35	$115,193.52	$168,248.30	$283,441.82
23	$76,716.22	$1,073.64	$753.99	$319.65	$124,037.77	$172,287.77	$296,325.54
24	$67,458.06	$1,073.64	$792.57	$281.08	$133,334.51	$175,874.75	$309,209.25
25	$57,726.23	$1,073.64	$833.12	$240.53	$143,106.89	$178,986.09	$322,092.97
26	$47,496.50	$1,073.64	$875.74	$197.90	$153,379.24	$181,597.46	$334,976.69
27	$36,743.41	$1,073.64	$920.55	$153.10	$164,177.14	$183,683.27	$347,860.41
28	$25,440.16	$1,073.64	$967.64	$106.00	$175,527.48	$185,216.65	$360,744.13
29	$13,558.61	$1,073.64	$1,017.15	$56.49	$187,458.53	$186,169.31	$373,627.85
30	$1,069.19	$1,073.64	$1,069.19	$4.45	$200,000.00	$186,511.57	$386,511.57

principal. The principal is the original amount of the loan. Table 3.1 displays an *amortization schedule* of a $200,000 30-year fixed mortgage with a 5% interest rate. An amortization schedule is a monthly or yearly table of loan payments that shows how much of your monthly payment goes towards interest and how much it reduces your loan balance. Take a look at the first few years of payments. Most of your money is going towards interest. Don't you wish you owned a bank! Remember, banks are not your friend. They are in the business to make money.

One interesting piece of data in Table 3.1 is the amount of the monthly payment that is applied to the principal in the later years of the loan. Your equity builds up much faster in years 16-30. However, most people do not live in their homes for thirty years. Homeowners usually own their properties for around 7-10 years. That means most of us will never have the opportunity to experience building equity quickly in this manner. You may be thinking to yourself that the 30-year rate doesn't sound like a smart financial decision. However, another advantage describes how you can deduct your mortgage interest from your income. This *can* be one of the best *tax deductions* you can claim, but **only** if your total itemized deductions exceeds the standard deduction. A tax deduction reduces your taxable income so that your tax liability is lower. For example, if your adjusted gross income is $100,000 and you have $35,000 in itemized deductions, your taxable income is now only $65,000 ($100,000 - $35,000). If your highest federal income tax rate is 22%, you will save $7,700 ($35,000 x 22%) in taxes.

Speaking of tax deductions, there is a significant difference between a tax deduction and a *tax credit* that everyone should clearly understand. A tax credit is a dollar for dollar reduction in your tax liability compared to a tax deduction which only reduces your taxes by a portion of the actual deduction. Table 3.2 clearly shows the effect that a $3,000 tax *deduction* versus a $3,000 tax *credit* will have on reducing your tax liability when assuming $70,000 in gross income and a 20% federal income tax rate. You can see that with a $3,000 tax credit, your tax liability is $2,400 less when compared to a $3,000 tax deduction. Obviously, tax credits are the better of the two, but are few and far between. Some examples of tax credits are the Child Tax Credit, the Earned Income Tax Credit, and the Lifetime Learning Credit. I highly recommend going to the irs.gov website to see if you qualify for any of these or other tax credits. A good accountant will also be knowledgeable on which credits you can take. I realize I went on a bit of a tangent, but I wanted to make sure you understand the key concepts that can make or save you money. We will now return to our regularly scheduled program...

Table 3.2

	$3,000 Tax Deduction	$3,000 Tax Credit
Gross Income	$70,000	$70,000
Tax Deduction	$3,000	$0
Taxable Income	$67,000	$70,000
Income Tax Rate	20%	20%
Taxes Owed	$13,400	$14,000
Tax Credit	$0	$3,000
FINAL Taxes Owed	**$13,400**	**$11,000**

One thing to consider is how much house you can afford. The general rule is to keep your monthly mortgage payment within 28% of your income, and preferably within 20-25%. Also, understand that your monthly payment will likely include real estate taxes and homeowners insurance. If your monthly payment exceeds these limitations, you run the risk of your home owning *you* rather than *you* owning your home. When house hunting, which can be enjoyable and exhausting at the same time, remember the general rule above. Many times potential homeowners get very excited about buying a home that is too big or expensive for their budgets. Instead of agreeing on a reasonably priced and decent-sized home, they get caught up in the euphoria of the home of their dreams, which can lead to unnecessary spending. It is similar to looking at new cars in the sense that it is very easy to overspend to get the next step up in style, space, and luxury. Also, you have to remember that a bigger house comes with higher utilities expenses, more furniture to fill up the space, and higher property taxes. And I haven't even mentioned the additional costs for any repairs. The bigger the house, the greater chance of more repairs.

Now let's discuss the 15-year fixed mortgage and how it compares to a 30-year mortgage. Some advantages of a 15-year fixed mortgage include:

- Borrowers build equity much quicker

- Overall interest paid to the bank is dramatically lower than those on longer-term loans
- Interest rates are lower than 30-year loans

Disadvantages of a 15-year fixed mortgage include:

- Monthly payments can be significantly higher than those on 30-year loans
- Restricts home buyers to smaller houses compared to what they might be able to afford with longer-term loans

One of the main reasons people choose a 15-year fixed mortgage is to build equity much faster. Table 3.3 compares the equity built up over a 15-year period on a $200,000 15-year mortgage at 5% to the first 15 years of a 30-year $200,000 mortgage at 5%. Incredible, wouldn't you agree?! In a perfect world, we would all be wise to choose a 15-year fixed mortgage, but we know the world is far from perfect. Notice the monthly payment in Table 3.3 for each loan. The payment for the 30-year mortgage is much lower than the 15-year mortgage, which is why most people choose the 30-year option.

Table 3.3

	15-Year $200,000 Mortgage			30-Year $200,000 Mortgage		
Year	Payment	Equity	Total Interest	Payment	Equity	Total Interest
1	$1,581.59	$9,187.70	$9,791.35	$1,073.64	$2,950.73	$9,932.99
2	$1,581.59	$18,845.46	$19,112.63	$1,073.64	$6,052.43	$19,715.01
3	$1,581.59	$28,997.34	$27,939.81	$1,073.64	$9,312.81	$29,338.35
4	$1,581.59	$39,668.60	$36,247.59	$1,073.64	$12,740.00	$38,794.87
5	$1,581.59	$50,885.82	$44,009.42	$1,073.64	$16,342.54	$48,076.06
6	$1,581.59	$62,676.93	$51,197.35	$1,073.64	$20,129.38	$57,172.93
7	$1,581.59	$75,071.31	$57,782.02	$1,073.64	$24,109.97	$66,076.06
8	$1,581.59	$88,099.80	$63,732.58	$1,073.64	$28,294.21	$74,775.54
9	$1,581.59	$101,794.85	$69,016.57	$1,073.64	$32,692.53	$83,260.94
10	$1,581.59	$116,190.57	$73,599.90	$1,073.64	$37,315.87	$91,521.32
11	$1,581.59	$131,322.81	$77,446.71	$1,073.64	$42,175.75	$99,545.16
12	$1,581.59	$147,229.23	$80,519.33	$1,073.64	$47,284.27	$107,320.35
13	$1,581.59	$163,949.46	$82,778.15	$1,073.64	$52,654.16	$114,834.19
14	$1,581.59	$181,525.13	$84,181.53	$1,073.64	$58,298.78	$122,073.29
15	$1,581.59	$200,000.00	$84,685.71	$1,073.64	$64,232.18	$129,023.60

However, if you can be satisfied with a smaller home and be comfortable with the higher monthly payment that doesn't exceed the general guidelines previously discussed, a 15-year mortgage can produce significant savings and potential wealth over the life of the loan.

A notable risk in 15-year fixed mortgages we need to discuss in more detail is the higher monthly payment. There is no flexibility when making your payments since they are fixed. If you lose your job, you may very well have difficulty paying on time, if at all. If you cannot afford to pay, you will incur late fees. Furthermore, if you fail to make payments over several months or more, you risk losing your home to foreclosure. That is a path you do not want to follow. This scenario is not to dissuade you from 15-year home loans, but rather to inform you of things to consider before choosing a mortgage.

Another method that builds equity faster, but also provides greater flexibility with your mortgage is to make extra payments on a 30-year loan. Table 3.4 shows the effect that an extra $250 payment per **month** can have on your principal and interest over the first

Table 3.4

		30-Year $250,000 Mortgage at 6%			
Year	Monthly Payments	Extra Monthly Payments	Cumulative Principal	Payment	Total Payments
1	$1,498.88	$250	$6,154	$14,833	$20,987
2	$1,498.88	$250	$12,687	$29,286	$41,973
3	$1,498.88	$250	$19,624	$43,336	$62,960
4	$1,498.88	$250	$26,988	$56,958	$83,946
5	$1,498.88	$250	$34,807	$70,126	$104,933
6	$1,498.88	$250	$43,107	$82,812	$125,919
7	$1,498.88	$250	$51,920	$94,986	$146,906
8	$1,498.88	$250	$61,276	$106,616	$167,892
9	$1,498.88	$250	$71,210	$117,669	$188,879
10	$1,498.88	$250	$81,756	$128,110	$209,866
11	$1,498.88	$250	$92,952	$137,900	$230,852
12	$1,498.88	$250	$104,839	$146,999	$251,839
13	$1,498.88	$250	$117,459	$155,366	$272,825
14	$1,498.88	$250	$130,858	$162,954	$293,812
15	$1,498.88	$250	$145,083	$169,715	$314,798

fifteen years of a $250,000 30-year loan at 6%. If you have the discipline to make the $250 extra payment every month, you can realize significant savings on interest similar to a 15-year loan because you are paying the loan off 9 years early. As a matter of fact, you would save almost $100,000 in interest over the life of the loan in this scenario! However, if you suffer a financial hardship, you can simply pay the required monthly amount and stop paying the extra money until your financial situation returns to normal. This is a fantastic option for many people who do not want to be locked into a higher monthly payment. I will tell you, however, that it is hard for many of us to be disciplined enough to consistently make extra payments. There always seems to be something else that comes up that you feel you need to buy.

Yet another way (albeit less common) to pay down a 30-year loan quicker is to pay half of your monthly payment every two weeks rather than one payment per month. The effect is basically the same as making one extra payment every year. For example, if your monthly mortgage payment is $2,000, you would make a $1,000 payment every two weeks instead of a $2,000 payment every month. Since there are 52 weeks in a year, you are paying a total of $26,000 ($1,000 x 26 weeks). You would only be paying a total of $24,000 in payments by just paying your mortgage once a month. Therefore, you are making an extra $2,000 payment every year by paying half every two weeks ($26,000 - $24,000).

The information and scenarios discussed are essential for you to comprehend in order to make informed decisions on an appropriate mortgage for your situation. It is also important to understand that managing your home loan in a responsible manner can lead to greater wealth in the long run. Home ownership provides a means of building wealth in the following ways:

- Building equity by paying down your principal
- Making extra payments that reduce your interest and speeds up the process of building equity
- Tax savings by deducting your mortgage interest and property taxes from your income
- Your home increasing in value over time which also leads to higher equity.

ADJUSTABLE-RATE MORTGAGES (ARMs)

Adjustable-rate mortgages (ARMs) are somewhat unique. ARMs are mortgage loans, usually with a term of 30 years, in which the interest rate is adjusted periodically (usually on an annual basis) *after* a specific period of fixed interest. The following list provides some examples of ARMs:

- 10/1-Fixed for 120 months, adjusts annually for the remaining term of the loan.
- 7/1-Fixed for 84 months, adjusts annually for the remaining term of the loan.
- 5/1-Fixed for 60 months, adjusts annually for the remaining term of the loan.
- 3/1-Fixed for 36 months, adjusts annually for the remaining term of the loan.

The first number represents the number of years the interest rate will stay the same. The second number represents how often the rate will potentially change. For example, a 7/1 ARM will have a fixed rate of interest for seven years. After the seven years, the rate becomes variable and can fluctuate on a yearly basis. Hence, the number one in 7/1. Every year your lender will determine the interest rate on your loan based on a number of factors, but essentially it will rise and fall depending on where overall rates are within the current economic environment. Additionally, you will find that the higher the fixed period, the higher the fixed interest rate. Therefore, a 10/1 ARM will have a fixed rate higher than a 7/1 ARM, the 7/1 ARM will have a higher fixed rate than a 5/1 ARM, and so on. Once the initial fixed period ends, monthly payments will vary each year for the remaining term of the loan. With a 7/1 ARM, your payment is fixed for seven years and the remaining 23 years will have variable payments. From a peace of mind perspective, ARMs would not be an appropriate choice. However, there are certainly some advantages of adjustable-rate mortgages including:

- Initial lower monthly payments
- Saving money
- Can afford a larger loan for a house
- Eliminate the need to refinance to obtain lower interest rates.

Disadvantages of adjustable-rate mortgages include:

- The risk that rates will rise on you
- Monthly payments can increase if rates rise
- May cost you more in the long run
- Difficult to devise a sustainable budget

One of the advantages above that is notable is the fact that ARMs usually have initial lower payments when compared to a 30-year fixed loan. That is because the interest rates on adjustable-rate mortgages are usually lower. Many young couples will consider ARMs for this reason alone. They may not have enough income yet to pay the higher interest rate of a conventional loan. An ARM will allow them to become homeowners and reap the benefits associated with home ownership.

Some people like ARMs because they simply want to save money during the initial fixed period. This can be a good way to find money to invest for your financial future. Of course, you need to be careful that your payments do not become a thorn in your side when the variable payment period begins and rears its ugly head. Adjustable-rate mortgages can also help you afford a larger house, but as always, be careful not to overextend your finances and become a slave to your home.

By now I am confident you are aware of the risks of adjustable-rate mortgages. However, it is important to remind you that most people do not live in their homes for more than ten years. Many people will find a new home in much less than ten years. There are many reasons for this including the fact that younger couples will need a larger home when they have children. Or maybe a family has to move elsewhere because they were relocated by their employer. Whatever the reason is, ARMs can be a wise choice if your plan is to move into a different home before the fixed period ends.

HOME EQUITY LOAN vs HOME EQUITY LINE OF CREDIT

Recall that home equity is defined as the difference between what your home is worth and the amount you owe on your mortgage. There are two main types of loans available to access the equity (or cash) in your home; a *Home Equity Loan* and a *Home Equity Line of Credit* (HELOC). Before diving into the attributes of each, I feel the need to make you aware of the dangers in using your home equity in ways that could be detrimental to your finances. You should NEVER use the equity in your home to purchase the following:

- Most investments including stocks
- Unnecessary products

- Your dream vacation
- Speculative real estate investments

Home equity can be useful to pay for things such as upgrades on your home or even college expenses if needed. Notice how I used the phrase "if needed". Ideally, your college expenses should be paid by using strategies discussed later in the book. As far as upgrading your home is concerned, many upgrades can increase the value of your home. For example, one of the best upgrades to your home you can make is the kitchen. Using your equity to upgrade your kitchen can be a smart use of your home equity because the money you spend can be made back by an increase in the value of your home.

A Home Equity Loan is simply a loan that borrows against the equity in your home. Using the previously discussed home equity example, if your home is valued at $300,000 and you owe $220,000 on your mortgage, you have $80,000 of equity. Therefore, you will likely be approved for a home equity loan that would allow you to access some of the $80,000 in equity. In this case, assuming you have a good credit score, you could probably take out a home equity loan of around $20,000. Usually, lenders will require that you maintain no less than 80% *loan-to-value*. Loan-to-value is a risk assessment ratio that banks and other lenders look at before approving a loan. Using our example, an 80% loan-to-value would be $240,000 ($300,000 x 80%). Since our mortgage balance in the example is $220,000, the maximum home equity loan that you could take would be $20,000 ($240,000 - $220,000). There are some lenders that will allow up to 90% loan-to-value, but I strongly discourage you from borrowing that much equity from your home.

Some advantages of a home equity loan include:

- Loan amount can be used however you wish

- Interest paid on the loan may be tax-deductible
- Home equity loan rates are usually lower than a personal loan from a bank

Disadvantages of a home equity loan include:

- You now have something similar to an additional mortgage on your home
- If you can't make the payments, it puts your home at risk for foreclosure
- Many home equity loans come with fees and closing costs
- Some home equity loans will charge you a fee for paying the loan off early

Home equity loans are fixed payments, similar to a 15 or 30-year fixed mortgage. You know what the payment will be and you have peace of mind knowing that it will never change.

A home equity line of credit, also known as a HELOC, functions much like a credit card. It is a form of revolving credit in which your home serves as collateral. In other words, you only use the available money on your HELOC when you need it. Similar to a credit card, you can pay it back in monthly payments or pay it back in full. For example, if you have a $20,000 HELOC, and you use $2,000 of it, you can make a minimum payment or pay back the entire $2,000 by the monthly due date. Also, in our example, if you use $2,000, you still have $18,000 available to use on your line of credit. One slight difference when compared to a credit card is that you are still charged interest on what you take out even if you pay it back in full by the first due date. However, the interest rates on HELOCs are usually much lower than interest rates on credit cards.

Some advantages of a HELOC include:

- Uses your most valuable asset in times of financial need
- You can borrow up to your credit limit whenever you want
- Interest paid on the loan may be tax deductible
- Interest rates are typically lower when compared to other forms of credit

Disadvantages of a HELOC include:

- Interest rates for HELOCs are variable meaning they can significantly rise over a period of time
- You now have something similar to an additional mortgage on your home
- If you can't make the payments, it puts your home at risk for foreclosure
- Some HELOCs come with fees and closing costs

Contrary to home equity loans, home equity lines of credit have variable payments because the payments are dependent on how much credit you use and how much the interest rate varies from month to month. It can be difficult to budget for variable payments since they can change over time and you may not have peace of mind knowing that they can become very high.

Home equity loans and lines of credit can be useful options that can help you manage your debt and provide an alternative source of funding for your needs. They can also be a good option if you find yourself swimming in a large pool of credit card debt. Obviously, you never want to be in that situation. However, if you are faced with this financial dilemma, a home equity loan or HELOC can be beneficial because you can pay off your high interest credit card balances while consolidating them into one loan with a lower rate.

REFINANCING YOUR MORTGAGE:
A GOOD OR BAD IDEA?

Congratulations to those of you who took advantage of historically low mortgage rates and refinanced your mortgage! I'm sure you are enjoying lower monthly payments or excited that you reduced the term of your loan. Hopefully, if you chose to enjoy lower monthly payments, you were responsible enough to save or invest your monthly savings. For readers who have yet to own a home or have recently bought a home, this section will help you understand the benefits of *refinancing* your mortgage. It will also help you determine *when* you should refinance. Refinancing means replacing your existing loan with a new loan that offers better rates or shorter term lengths. Refinancing is another way to increase your cash flow and can be a smart way to propel your drive to financial success. The following is a list of the possible benefits enjoyed by homeowners after refinancing their mortgage:

- Lower monthly payment
- Building equity in their home at a faster rate
- Debt consolidation
- Accessing the equity in their home for various reasons
- The ability to shorten the loan length to pay it off faster

While all of the benefits above are significant, two of them in particular stand out. Debt consolidation is a powerful strategy for people who have piled on excessive debt through credit cards or other types of loans. Refinancing can allow homeowners to use the equity in their homes to pay off high-interest loan balances. The result is that the homeowner now has just one loan to pay back and will likely have a more reasonable interest rate which saves them money in the long run. Ideally, you never want to be in that situation. However, it is good to know that you have options to help you in that set of circumstances.

The other benefit that I find intriguing is accessing the equity in your home to purchase another asset that can help create long-term wealth. I'll use a real-life example of how this can be useful. My wife and I refinanced our home and used the equity to purchase another home a few towns away from where we reside. We used the cash for the down payment as well as the repairs needed on the house. After spending about three months fixing it up, we began renting it out. The rent we receive pays our monthly mortgage payment and also provides us with a few hundred dollars of increased cash flow. We are also building equity in the home and can deduct the mortgage interest from our income. I would like to note that not everyone has success when purchasing an investment property. I have heard nightmare stories of renters who destroy houses or refuse to pay the rent. We were certainly lucky that we found a very good tenant.

Generally speaking, if current mortgage rates are a full percent lower than yours, it is a good idea to refinance. For example, if your mortgage rate is 6% and comparable rates have gone down to 5%, you should probably refinance. There are, of course, some caveats. If you have owned your home for a long time and are getting close to paying off your loan entirely, you do not need to refinance. Furthermore, if you are planning on moving within the next few years, refinancing likely won't be feasible. This is because there can be many loan fees when refinancing, similar to the closing costs when taking out an initial mortgage when you purchase a home. Some of these fees include, but are not limited to:

- Origination fee
- Appraisal fee
- Credit report

- Flood certification
- Recording fee
- Title insurance
- Escrow fees
- Tax fees

As you can see, these costs can cause you to think twice about refinancing. That is why you should calculate the amount of time it takes to break even on your new loan. In other words, how long will it take you to recuperate the costs of refinancing? This is sometimes called the *recovery period*. To calculate the recovery period, figure out how much lower your monthly payments will be with the comparable lower rate. Then divide your closing costs by the amount you will be saving monthly. The result will tell you how many months it will take to recover the costs of the loan. After you get past the recovery period, you will begin to benefit from the monthly savings. Let's take a look at a typical refinancing example.

After living in your first home for five years, you find that mortgage rates have declined. Your current mortgage is for 30 years and has a 7% interest rate. Now, the same 30-year mortgage consists of a 5 ½ % interest rate. Therefore, you decide to take the plunge and go through the tedious process of applying for a refinanced loan. And yes, the process can be quite cumbersome, deterring many people from ever doing it. I can honestly say that the time and effort is well worth it from a financial perspective! Moving along, you understand that you need to look at the numbers and figure out how long it will take to break even when considering the closing costs you will need to pay. You discover that refinancing your mortgage will save you about $250 each month from your monthly payment. However, the closing costs add up to approximately $6,000. Doing a simple calculation of $6,000 divided by $250, you come up with an answer of 24. This means that it will take about 24 months to recover the closing costs. After 24 months, you will begin to reap the benefits of your new loan, and can use those savings in ways that increase your long-term wealth. Knowing that you are planning on living in your home for at least the next five years, you pull the trigger and call your bank or mortgage broker and begin filling out all of the annoying forms. You should congratulate yourself though, and be thrilled that you are taking advantage of this golden opportunity.

There is another situation that presents an opportunity to refinance. Any homeowner who has an adjustable rate mortgage that is about to have the fixed rate period expire should consider refinancing. In most cases, when your fixed rate expires, the new variable rate will be higher. Refinancing to a fixed rate mortgage could be advantageous because of the potential lower rate. Of course my suggestion is that you check current mortgage rates on the Internet before going through the process. If fixed-rate mortgages are higher than the variable rate, it wouldn't make sense to refinance. Some useful sites to find current mortgage rates include Bankrate.com and Mortgagenewsdaily.com.

Choosing a home loan should be an essential part of your long-term financial plan. Owning a home and managing a mortgage responsibly is an important component of building wealth. Remember to take a step back and choose a home and a home loan that is appropriate for your financial situation. You should be able to live comfortably *in* your home, not live *for* your home.

Key Points to Remember from Chapter 3

- Owning a home can build equity and create wealth
- Choose a home that fits your family's needs, not one that breaks your bank account
- Beware of lenders offering low down payment mortgages

- Make sure your monthly payment does not exceed 28% of your income
- Utilize methods to pay off your loan quicker, reducing your overall interest paid
- Only use a home equity loan or HELOC when necessary
- Refinance your loan when appropriate to benefit from lower rates

CHAPTER FOUR

How Much Will I Need to Save to Retire Comfortably?

In this chapter we will talk about the importance of retirement planning including how much of a nest egg you will need to have. Let's discuss the strategies that help us save enough money for our golden years. There are several key items you need to consider before you can determine how much money you'll need in order to fund your retirement. These include the following:

- Decide the age at which you want to retire
- Decide the annual income you'll need for your retirement years
- Determine a conservative annual rate of return on your investments (I recommend using 6% or 7%)
- Use a conservative *post*-retirement annual rate of return (3%-4% but depends on the current interest-rate environment)
- Conservatively assume inflation will be somewhere between 3% to 4% annually

When deciding the age you would like to retire, please do not be unrealistic. Yes, there are people who have retired at an incredibly early age, but most of us will need to work for four to five decades. That sure does sound like a long time, but it goes very quick! If you do want to retire at an earlier age (let's say 55), then you need to plan accordingly. You will need to make sure you have enough money to provide the investment income required for you to retire comfortably. Let's take a look at some useful calculations to help us determine how much we need to invest for a comfortable retirement.

Many people save or invest their money on a regular basis. *Periodic Investment Plans* are when you save or invest the same amount at regular intervals (such as monthly, weekly, or biweekly). Our first calculation that will help us is called *Future Value* of a periodic investment. Future Value is the value your account grows to at some point in the future. For example:

Rich, 30 years old, opens up an investment account and sets up a periodic investment plan. He plans to save $5,000 each year in the account until he reaches age 50. Assuming his investments return an average of 6% per year and are compounded annually, how much will he have in his account at age 50?

The first thing you may notice about the question above is the fact that Rich is assuming an average return per year of 6%. Most of us realize that his investment account will not return exactly 6% per year. Some years his investments may return much higher than 6% while other years he may lose money. However, the stock market has historically returned an average of about 10% per year. Having said that, there are *no* guarantees when it comes to investing, but 6% is a reasonable rate of return to expect over the long-term.

The formula we can use for the future value of a periodic investment is as follows:

$$B = \frac{P\left[\left(1 + \frac{r}{n}\right)^{nt} - 1\right]}{\left(\frac{r}{n}\right)}$$

Do not let the formula scare you! It really is quite simple. Let's define the variables:

B = balance at end of investment period (or Future Value)
P = periodic deposit amount
r = annual interest rate expressed as a decimal
n = number of times interest is compounded annually
t = length of investment in years

Substituting the numbers for the variables we get the following:

$B = 5,000((1 + .06/1)^{1(20)} - 1)/(.06 \div 1)$

Calculating the numbers using the order of operations (remember **PEMDAS**, or 'Please Excuse My Dear Aunt Sally', or **Parenthesis** first, then **Exponents, Multiplication, Division, Addition,** and finally **Subtraction**), our answer is approximately $183,925. Therefore, Rich might have around $183,925 in twenty years if he invests $5,000 per year while earning 6% annual returns on his investments. Hopefully, you can see the usefulness of the future value calculation. It can give you an idea of how much you may have at some point in the future when investing periodically.

The next calculation we can use is essentially the opposite of the future value of a periodic investment. This time we will figure out how much we need to save or invest *per period* to reach a financial goal. For this calculation we use the *Present Value of a periodic investment*. The formula we can use for the present value of a periodic investment is as follows:

$$P = \frac{B\left(\dfrac{r}{n}\right)}{\left(1 + \dfrac{r}{n}\right)^{nt} - 1}$$

The variables in this formula represent the same numbers as the future value formula:

B = balance at end of investment period
P = periodic deposit amount
r = annual interest rate expressed as a decimal
n = number of times interest is compounded annually
t = length of investment in years

Let's see how we can use the present value of a periodic deposit formula to figure out how much we need to deposit on a monthly basis to reach a specific goal:

Randy wants to have saved a total of $200,000 twenty years from now. He is willing to set up a direct deposit account with a 4.5% APR, compounded monthly. Calculate the amount per deposit Randy has to make for the 20 years if he makes monthly deposits.

The first thing you may notice about this particular question is the fact that Randy is assuming an average interest rate of 4.5%. As of this writing, interest rates on deposit accounts aren't even close to 4.5%. However, you can use this formula when investing in stocks as well as other investments. Therefore, a 4.5% rate of return is actually very conservative, although *never* guaranteed.

Substituting the numbers for the variables we get the following:

$$P = 200,000(.045/12)/(1 + .045/12)^{12(20)} - 1$$

Calculating the numbers using the order of operations, our answer is approximately $515. Therefore, Randy needs to save or invest about $515 each month for twenty years at an annual rate of return of 4.5% to reach his goal of $200,000. Hopefully, Randy's $515 each month can grow to more than $200,000 over the next twenty years!

Most, if not all, of us will need a heck of a lot more than $200,000 to retire comfortably. Given the uncertainty of Social Security, the disappearance of corporate pensions, the public pension crisis, and the ongoing effects of inflation and other economic factors, many of us will probably need to have several million dollars or more. That certainly sounds like an unattainable goal, but with proper planning and early investing it is definitely possible. The main reason why we need a large nest egg is because we need to generate enough income from our investments to replace the income we will no longer receive from our jobs. Yes, in retirement we *may* have less expenses. The general rule is that we should plan on replacing about 80% of your pre-retirement income. However, some of us, including my wife and I, plan on traveling to many parts of the world in our retirement years. Even traveling domestically will require more of our retirement income and proper planning.

Before taking a look at some basic examples of how much income our investments might generate in retirement, we need to make a conservative assumption of our *post*-retirement return we will have from our investments. In other words, what is a reasonable annual rate of return of *income* we can expect to receive from our investments? Keep in mind that in retirement we are no longer in the 'accumulation' phase, but are now in the 'income' phase. We hopefully have already grown our savings and investments enough to live off of the income we receive from them in the form of interest, dividends, and capital gains. A reasonable annual rate of return of income we can expect would be around 4%. Please realize, however, that 4% might be considered too conservative or even too aggressive for some people. Interest rates are historically low as of this writing, but maybe rates will go higher in the future (which is very likely), affecting rates on certain investments. In that case, we might raise our assumption and use 4.5% or even 5%. Regardless of where interest rates are at the time of retirement, the most important thing to remember is to be **conservative** in our assumptions. Being conservative in our assumptions will reduce the risk of not having enough retirement income to live comfortably. In the past, I have actually used a 3.5% annual rate of return of income when calculating a client's projected retirement income. Finally, let's take a look at a basic example of projected retirement income:

John and Clare just retired and have accumulated about $2,000,000 in savings and investments. Assuming a post-retirement return of 4%, they can expect an annual income of approximately $80,000 ($2,000,000 X 4%). That's it! It's that simple! Of course, John and Clare did proper planning and understand that they can live comfortably on $80,000 per year and will also receive social security benefits at some point. Furthermore, they realize that inflation will eat into their annual income, so they needed to plan accordingly. They understand that the $80,000 in income they need could have a future value of around $113,000 or more after ten years when factoring in annual inflation. Some of their investments, however, provide a hedge (protection) against inflation. We will be discussing some of these investments in Chapter 5. Also, be aware that not *every* expense will rise with inflation. For example, if you still have a fixed mortgage payment when you retire, the principal and interest portion of the payment remains constant.

The $2,000,000 that John and Clare accumulated is considered their principal amount. The principal amount should *never* be used to fund their retirement. I could certainly go on a tangent for many hours on why no one should use their principal to fund their retirement. The short answer is that we have no idea how long we will live in retirement. However, with all of the medical advances, many of us will live 25 years or more in retirement, fueling the need to make certain we have enough annual income.

There is also a way to 'back into' the amount of money we need to have saved for retirement. Let's assume that we have calculated our annual retirement income needed as $100,000. Let's also assume a conservative post-retirement annual rate of return of 3.5%. We simply divide $100,000 by 3.5% (or $100,000 divided by .035) and get approximately $2,857,143. That is the amount of money we would need when we retire to generate $100,000 per year in income assuming a 3.5% post-retirement return. Table 4.1 provides the amount of principal needed when we retire based on various income needs and post-retirement rate of returns:

Table 4.1

Income Needed in Retirement	Post-Retirement Rate of Return	Principal Needed
$75,000	3.50%	$2,142,857
$75,000	4.00%	$1,875,000
$75,000	4.50%	$1,666,667
$100,000	3.50%	$2,857,143
$100,000	4.00%	$2,500,000
$100,000	4.50%	$2,222,222
$125,000	3.50%	$3,571,429
$125,000	4.00%	$3,125,000
$125,000	4.50%	$2,777,778
$150,000	3.50%	$4,285,714
$150,000	4.00%	$3,750,000
$150,000	4.50%	$3,333,333

The principal amount needed in retirement is unique for everyone and quite possibly could change throughout your career based on many factors. However, it is an important number to use as a retirement goal and to motivate you to plan and invest early. When deciding on how much you will need, it is important to revisit your budget and include every expense you will likely have in your golden years. Some of these expenses can include travel, gifts for children and grandchildren, prescriptions, entertainment, dining out, and many others. Please do not forget to be conservative in your budget items. It is ALWAYS better to overestimate your expenses rather than underestimate them so there are no surprises down the road.

Finally, one major expense in retirement you should never forget is your health care premiums for you and your significant other. This is especially important for anyone retiring prior to age 65, when Medicare kicks in and pays for your *basic* health needs. Most people do not have access to free healthcare benefits in retirement before 65. Shockingly, many people do not realize that they will likely need $25,000 or more *per year* to pay for healthcare benefits until Medicare begins. Even after Medicare begins, there are many health-related expenses that you will need to pay. Therefore, it is important to acknowledge that healthcare will definitely be a significant portion of your overall annual expenses and to be careful not to underestimate the cost.

Saving enough for retirement is *our* responsibility. There is no 'politically correct' way of stating this fact. Please do not buy into the notion that our government will take care of us. It is highly unlikely that the United States government will have enough resources in the future to hand out full entitlements to all of its citizens. Be proactive and take control of your financial future by planning and investing early. And remember, failing to plan means planning to fail!

Key Points to Remember from Chapter 4

- Assume a conservative rate of return on your investments (6% or 7%)

- Assume a conservative post-retirement rate of return
- Use the periodic investment formulas to determine how much you will need to invest
- Analyze your budget needs for retirement to figure out how much income you will need
- Plan for inflation affecting the amount of income you will need in subsequent retirement years
- Understand that healthcare costs can be a significant portion of your retirement expenses
- Failing to plan means planning to fail

CHAPTER FIVE

INVESTMENTS 101

Mark likes to live for the moment. At 52 years old, he and his family have spent most of their moderate income buying depreciating assets. Mark has never worried about retirement until now. He finally realizes that he will not be able to stop working unless he accumulates a significant amount of money in a very short period of time. After meeting with a financial advisor, Mark is shocked, to say the least, at the reality he now faces. All of his hard work over his career has amounted to a grand total of $8,000 in savings and understands that retiring at a reasonable age is highly unlikely. If he is fortunate enough to keep his job at a much older age, he is looking at working well into his 70's just to meet his basic needs. Yes, social security will be there in some capacity, but certainly not enough to enjoy his later years in life. How did this happen? Why didn't Mark listen to his Wealth Management teacher, Mr. Zisa, about the benefits of investing early?! Life went so fast!

Unfortunately, the above scenario is not uncommon. Most people put off saving and investing until it is too late. Consequently, many people that are 'retired' have part-time or full-time jobs just to keep their heads above water. Think about how many elderly people you know that are working just because they need the income. Quite frankly, I feel for many of them because they cannot enjoy their remaining years as they were led to believe. I realize that some older people simply want to work because it makes them happy to do something of importance or to just keep busy. I sincerely respect that decision and I may find myself feeling the same way when I retire. However, for those of us who do not want to be in Mark's situation, this chapter will explain to you how to utilize specific investments and retirement accounts to help you on your path to financial success and a happy retirement. Please keep in mind that before saving and investing *any* of your hard-earned money, you should be relatively debt free. I use the word "relatively" because having a mortgage on your home is a necessity for most of us. Debt free means not having any unnecessary debt such as credit card balances or other high-rate loans. Pay them off as fast as you can in order to begin to invest and grow your wealth.

STOCKS (a.k.a. EQUITIES)

I'm sure by now you have heard of *stocks*. When you invest in (or buy) a stock, you are actually part owner of the company! Your portion of the company will be very small, but there are advantages with being an owner such as:

- You are entitled to a portion of the profits in the form of dividends (companies may not always be in a position to pay dividends)
- You have voting rights (one vote for every share of stock you own)

Stocks can be volatile (risky) and, therefore, should be considered long-term investments. A major disadvantage of investing in a stock is that you assume all of the risk associated with being an owner. If the company goes out of business, you could lose all of your money. However, from a historical perspective, stocks have gone up an average of approximately 10% a year. There is certainly no guarantee that stocks will continue to rise on a long-term basis, but it is important to have them in your investment *portfolio* given their historical success. A portfolio is a grouping of financial assets (or investments) such as stocks, bonds, mutual funds, exchange-traded funds (ETFs), and cash equivalents.

A stock *dividend* is the profit that a company earns and shares with the owners. Imagine that! Simply for owning certain stocks, you will receive profit from the company for doing absolutely nothing. Now, let's say you own 100 shares of XYZ company. Let's also assume that XYZ pays a $2 dividend per share every year. That means that every year you will receive $200 in dividends from XYZ. What can you do with that $200? You have two options:

1. Take the dividends as cash
2. Reinvest the dividends into more shares of the company

If you take the $200 as cash, you can spend it as you wish. If you take the $200 and reinvest it into more shares of XYZ stock, you may receive more in dividends in the future. This is a form of compounding. As long as we own XYZ stock, and as long as we keep reinvesting the dividends, our investment should continue to compound over the years. Table 5.1 on the next page shows dividend reinvesting when investing $2,500 in a company that pays a 4% dividend per share. The table also assumes the dividend increases 5% per year and the price per share rises an average of 8% each year. While the increase in dividends and stock prices are never guaranteed, some companies do raise their dividends in many years. However, it is worth noting that there are no assurances that any company will pay, let alone increase, its dividend payment.

Table 5.1*

Year	# Shares Owned	Price per Share	Dividend per Share	Annual Dividend Amount	Total Stock Value
1	100	$25.00	$1.00	$100	$2,500
2	104	$27.00	$1.05	$109	$2,804
3	108	$29.16	$1.10	$119	$3,141
4	112	$31.49	$1.16	$129	$3,516
5	116	$34.01	$1.22	$141	$3,932
6	120	$36.73	$1.28	$153	$4,392
7	124	$39.67	$1.34	$166	$4,902
8	128	$42.85	$1.41	$180	$5,466
9	132	$46.27	$1.48	$194	$6,090
10	136	$49.98	$1.55	$210	$6,779
11	140	$53.97	$1.63	$228	$7,539
12	144	$58.29	$1.71	$246	$8,379
13	148	$62.95	$1.80	$265	$9,305
14	152	$67.99	$1.89	$286	$10,324
15	156	$73.43	$1.98	$309	$11,448
16	160	$79.30	$2.08	$333	$12,684
17	164	$85.65	$2.18	$358	$14,044
18	168	$92.50	$2.29	$385	$15,539
19	172	$99.90	$2.41	$414	$17,182
20	176	$107.89	$2.53	$445	$18,987
21	180	$116.52	$2.65	$477	$20,968
22	184	$125.85	$2.79	$512	$23,141
23	188	$135.91	$2.93	$549	$25,524
24	192	$146.79	$3.07	$589	$28,137
25	196	$158.53	$3.23	$631	$30,999
26	199	$171.21	$3.39	$675	$34,134
27	203	$184.91	$3.56	$722	$37,565
28	207	$199.70	$3.73	$773	$41,321
29	211	$215.68	$3.92	$826	$45,429
30	214	$232.93	$4.12	$882	$49,920

Note: The above chart is for hypothetical illustration. There is no guarantee that a company will pay or increase their dividend.

Advantages of Stocks

- Higher **POTENTIAL** return
- Some stocks pay dividends
- The ability to reinvest dividends and take advantage of compounding
- Voting rights

Disadvantages of Stocks

- Stocks are riskier investments
- In theory, you can lose all of your money
- Stocks can be volatile and unpredictable

Real-Life Application

Emily, 27, and Dave, 28, are newly married and decide they would like to begin investing in dividend-paying stocks to get a head start on their retirement savings. Emily is going to graduate school next year, but plans on working part-time during the school year. Dave has a full-time job as a computer programmer. Their combined income will be about $65,000. Emily needs to budget for her tuition and books next year and estimates it will cost her about $7,000 for the year. Consider the following question about Emily & Dave's situation:

- *Should Emily & Dave invest ALL of their money in stocks this year?*

Options & Considerations:
- Any money for a goal that has a time frame of less than 5 years (also known as short-term goals) should be kept in savings because investing the money is too risky. Therefore, they could take $7,000 this year and put it in short-term savings for Emily's graduate school expenses. A savings account that pays interest or a short-term certificate of deposit (CD) may make sense.

BONDS

When you invest in (or buy) a bond, you are NOT an owner, but a lender (creditor). You loan your money to a company or government. They are designed to pay you back back with interest (every 6 months) over a specified period of time. In general, highly-rated bonds are less volatile than stocks, and therefore, less risky. Your earnings are predictable and you will receive a higher interest rate than what you would get in a typical bank account. Main types of bonds include:

- **U.S. Government Bonds**-(bills, notes, & bonds), extremely safe, therefore, lower interest rates
- **Municipal Bonds**-interest is free from federal income taxes, issued by local and state governments
- **Corporate Bonds**-can be riskier, but usually offer higher interest rates, issued by many companies

Bonds are considered *fixed-income* investments and can be good for your short-term goals if you invest in a short-term bond. Fixed-income investments can balance your portfolio while providing you with a specific amount of income. One major disadvantage of a bond is that you likely will not make as much money over a long period of time when compared to stocks. However, bonds are typically less volatile and can help to reduce the overall risk of your investment portfolio.

<u>Advantages of Bonds</u>

- Less risky when compared to stocks
- Predictable returns
- Can be good for short-term goals
- Creates balance in your portfolio and may help to reduce overall risk

Disadvantages of Bonds

- In general, returns are lower than stocks over the long term
- If the company or government can't pay back the money to bondholders, you can lose your entire investment

Examples of Investing in Bonds

- You want to save for a down payment for a new car in four years so you invest in a corporate bond that pays an interest rate (also known as the coupon) of 3% and ends in four years (also known as the maturity date), which is when you are paid back the face value of the bond (the amount that was loaned).
- You have been very successful and are making a large salary at your job. However, your large salary triggers huge federal income taxes. Therefore, you decide to invest in some municipal bonds, which are free from federal income taxes.
- You investment portfolio is worth $30,000 and consists of all stocks. You have $5,000 more to invest and you decide to buy more stocks because of their higher POTENTIAL return.

Real-Life Application

Jeff and his wife, Aimee, are looking to buy their first home in a few years and need to save money for a down payment. Their savings account is only paying them .25% interest on their money. They are considering investing in stocks to accumulate the funds they need for the down payment. Their combined income is about $60,000. Consider the following questions about Jeff and Aimee's situation:

- *Should Jeff and Aimee simply put money in their savings account for the down payment?*

- *Is it a good idea for them to invest in stocks for the down payment?*

Options & Considerations:

▪ Putting money in their savings account is not a terrible idea and is very safe. However, given that the inflation rate averages around 3% a year, their REAL RATE OF RETURN is -2.75% (.25% minus 3.00%). Jeff and Aimee may wish to consider other investment options.

▪ Investing in stocks for the short-term is extremely risky. They may wish to consider bonds that have a shorter maturity--no more than 3 years since that is when they will need the money. Additionally, since they do not have a large income and are not in a high tax bracket, they may wish to look at corporate bonds that have a high credit rating. The tax-free earnings from municipal bonds may not benefit them.

The concepts in these chapters are meant to address common financial concepts and strategies. The views and opinions expressed throughout are those of the author, are subject to change based on market and other various events, and are not meant as specific individualized advice. Please understand that all investing involves risk, including the loss of principal and that no strategy can guarantee a positive return or protect against loss. None of the content of this book is meant to replace specific tax or legal counsel from a licensed or qualified professional.

Investors should be aware that mutual funds, ETFs and variable annuities are sold by a prospectus which explains the objectives of the fund along with the risks, fees, and other charges associated with an investment in the fund. Investors should always read the prospectus carefully to understand the features and risks before investing. Your financial advisor and the Fund Company must make these documents available to you at your request.

MUTUAL FUNDS

A *mutual fund* is an investment that can consist of all stocks, all bonds, or a mixture of various types of investments. Since mutual funds can include multiple investments, they are naturally diversified (and usually less risky) than owning an individual stock. They are *actively-managed*, meaning they have managers and analysts working on your behalf to buy and sell investments within the fund. Because they are actively-managed, they may outperform the average investor trying to invest in individual stocks themselves. However, mutual funds carry ongoing annual expenses, known as the *expense ratio*, not found when owning individual stocks. The expense ratio is the annual percentage that is taken out of your mutual fund to pay for fees including marketing, commissions, and management fees. The average expense ratio for actively-managed mutual funds is around 1.50%. These fees can significantly affect the performance of your mutual fund over the long run.

Any dividends or capital gains you receive from a mutual fund are subject to taxes, even if you reinvest them into more shares of the fund, unless you hold them within a tax-advantaged retirement account. Capital gains fall under two categories; short-term and long-term. Short-term capital gains are generated from investments held for less than one year and are taxed based on your federal income tax rate. Long-term capital gains are generated from investments held for more than one year and are taxed at a flat rate, usually lower than what you would pay on short-term capital gains. It is important to note that other types of investments may be taxed as well. For example, dividends from individual stocks are taxed. Also, selling an individual stock for a profit will incur short-term or long-term capital gains if not in a tax-advantaged retirement account.

It is important to have a solid understanding of mutual funds since there is a very good chance you will be investing in them. That is because most employers offer retirement plans (mainly 401k plans) that only allow you to invest in mutual funds. We'll discuss 401k plans later in the chapter.

Advantages of Mutual Funds*

- Professional management
- Diversification
- Very liquid (easy to sell)
- Simplicity

Disadvantages of Mutual Funds

- Can have high annual fees
- Potential **OVER**-diversification
- Fund managers do not manage the fund according to your individual tax situation

Note: As with any investment that carries risk, you may lose money, including your principal investment

Real-Life Application

Mark, 25, wants to start investing about $100 per month in stocks to get a head start on generating wealth. He opens up an investment account and begins putting $100 in each month automatically from his savings account. Each month he invests about $50 of the money to buy stock while paying a $9.99 commission each time. He also wants to invest in bonds to diversify, but realizes he must wait to accumulate a large amount of cash to buy a bond. Consider the following questions about Mark's situation:

- Is it wise for Mark to buy $50 worth of stock each month from his $100 he is adding to his account?
- Should Mark wait to accumulate enough money to buy an individual bond?

Options & Considerations:

- Each time Mark buys $50 worth of stock he is paying $9.99. That can be a losing method of investing because he has already lost almost 20% of his investment. Although there may be transaction charges and fees associated with a mutual fund as well as possible account minimums, Mark should consider investing $50 a month into a stock mutual fund. As a small investor, a mutual fund can provide him the ability to diversify his portfolio.
- If Mark wants to further diversify by purchasing bonds, he should invest in a bond mutual fund, which he can afford to do right away with the other $50 he has per month.

INDEX FUNDS

Index funds are another type of mutual fund that we need to spend some time discussing in greater detail. First, let's define the term *index*. An index is a statistical measure of the changes in a portfolio of stocks, or other investments, representing a segment of the overall market. Essentially, an index is just a list of companies represented in a particular segment of the market. Some of the major stock indexes include:

- DJIA (Dow Jones Industrial Average)
- S&P 500 (Standard & Poor's 500 Index)

- NASDAQ Composite Index
- Wilshire 5000 Total Market Index
- Russell 2000 Index

The Dow Jones Industrial Average is the oldest index which consists of 30 companies known as "blue chips" that have a long history of consistent earnings and have an excellent reputation for delivering profit in both good and bad economic times. This is why many investors consider the DJIA to be a low-risk index. Furthermore, the 30 companies in the DJIA are considered leaders in their respective industries. Since these companies generate consistent earnings, they generally pay solid dividends.

The S&P 500 is a broader index that lists the 500 most widely held companies in the United States and therefore is considered to be one of the better measurements on how the overall market is doing on a daily, monthly, and annual basis. Because it contains 500 companies, it is well-diversified and accounts for a large percentage of the U.S. stock market. It is also the index that many investors use to compare their investment portfolio performance against and provides a benchmark for mutual fund managers. All of the stocks listed in the Dow Jones Industrial Average can be found in the S&P 500.

The NASDAQ Composite Index contains over 3,000 companies, with many being technology, Internet, and smaller companies. Technology and Internet companies tend to be more volatile given the nature of their businesses. Consequently, the NASDAQ is considered to be an index that is riskier and is watched by investors that have a higher risk tolerance. Conversely, the NASDAQ lists companies that have the potential to grow at a much faster pace when compared to the Dow Jones Industrial Average.

The Wilshire 5000 Total Market Index is a list of almost every public company in the United States and is thus the most diversified index around. However, because it only lists stocks from the United States, there are many foreign companies that are left out. It is interesting to note that the Wilshire 5000 actually lists over 6,000 companies, unlike its name would suggest.

The Russell 2000 Index consists of 2,000 of the smaller companies in the United States that have high growth potential. In periods of good economic times, companies within the Russell 2000 have experienced above-average gains in the stock market. Conversely, when economic times are tough, many of these smaller stocks fall dramatically and may even go out of business. The main reason that smaller companies have significant issues in a bad economy is because it is much more difficult to have enough available cash to make it through a rough period. Larger companies can withstand tougher economic times because they usually have a broader range of goods and services to fall back on, and typically have more cash in reserves for emergency purposes.

Other indexes include non-U.S. indexes and industry or sector indexes. Similar types of indexes are in all of the major countries in the world. For example, the Nikkei is Japan's main index, the Hang Seng is China's main index, and the DAX is Germany's main index. Sector indexes are simply indexes that list companies from a specific industry. There are sector indexes for almost all industries including, but not limited to, healthcare, retail, utilities, education, financial services, transportation, and even mining. Index funds* are just mutual funds! There are hundreds of indexes and hundreds of index funds. However, there are a couple of important facts about investing in index funds:

- They are passively-managed, not actively-managed
- They generally have lower fees/expenses than actively-managed mutual funds

Think of what passively-managed versus actively-managed could mean relevant to mutual funds. Remember that most mutual funds have managers that buy and sell investments within their fund for the benefit of the shareholder. Also, recall that these managers and their team get paid quite a bit of money to manage their fund. This is why mutual funds that are managed on a day-to-day basis are considered actively-managed. Now think about an index fund and how it operates. Would an index fund require day-to-day management like an actively-managed fund? Of course not! Although there is always some form of management for every mutual fund, there is limited management for index funds because they just track an index. Therefore, index funds are considered to be passively-managed.

We know that ALL mutual funds have an expense ratio which includes costs for the fund managers, advertising and other expenses. Since index funds are passively-managed, their expense ratios are much lower than actively-managed funds. Lower expense ratios help us keep more of our returns because the fund expenses do not eat into our gains. It is astonishing to realize that many actively-managed funds do not beat the overall returns of the stock market over a long period of time! One of the main reasons is because of their higher expense ratios, although certainly not the only reason. Many actively-managed funds might perform better in some years, but be careful you do not chase the latest and so-called greatest investment because it had one or two stellar years.

*Index performance does not reflect the deduction of any fees and expenses, and if deducted, performance would be reduced. Index funds are unmanaged and investors are not able to invest directly into any index.

Real-Life Application

Kayla and Mark, recently married, want to start building wealth for the long-term. They have conservative personalities when it comes to investing. They also do not have the time to research various types of investments given their busy schedule between attending night classes and their full-time jobs. They open up an investment account and begins putting $100 in each month automatically from their checking account. Consider the following questions about Kayla and Mark's situation:

- Is it wise for Kayla and Mark to invest in individual stocks and bonds?
- Should they invest in mutual funds instead?
- Should they invest in index funds?

Options and Considerations:
- Kayla and Mark may be better off staying away from individual stocks and bonds given their conservative personalities. They do not want to worry about daily fluctuations in the prices of a few investments.
- Mutual funds are certainly an option, but index funds may be more suitable for their unique situation because they do not have much time or the desire to analyze actively-managed funds.
- A possible strategy for Kayla and Mark may be to invest in inexpensive index funds that require a minimal amount of research and time. They will still be able to grow their investment portfolio over a long period of time, but without having to worry about their investments as much.

EXCHANGE-TRADED FUNDS (ETFs)

Exchange-traded funds are becoming increasingly popular among investors. However, like any investment, ETFs have positives and negative attributes. An Exchange-Traded Fund (ETF) is an investment that tracks an index, a commodity or a group of assets much like an index fund, but trades like a stock. ETFs, like index funds, are passively-managed.

ETFs have become popular because they generally do not come with the same annual expenses like actively-managed mutual funds. In fact, since they trade like stocks, the only expense you pay will be for the cost of the trade. However, it is important to note that some ETFs are leveraged. Being a leveraged ETF indicates that they are borrowing money to buy more investments. To illustrate this concept, let's look at a real-life example.

As previously stated, my wife and I decided to purchase an investment property. Since we did not have the cash at the time to afford the down payment, we took cash, or equity, out of our home. Recall, we did this by refinancing our home loan. Taking equity from our home resulted in a higher mortgage balance, which is certainly a risky thing to do. However, we used that cash to buy another asset; the investment property. We now own two homes, one which we rent out, and one that we live in. To summarize, we leveraged the equity in our home to buy the investment property. We subsequently increased our risk, but furthered our chances of potentially higher gains. Although this is not exactly the same as purchasing leveraged ETFs, the basic concept is similar. These types of complex products may not be suitable for beginning investors.

Like mutual funds, ETFs offer inherent diversification within your portfolio since they are comprised of numerous investments.

Another similarity to mutual funds is that you can invest in a particular sector or industry of the market. For example, there are ETFs that will allow you to gain exposure to the oil service industry or even the gold mining industry. These ETFs can be riskier because you are only invested in one area of the economy. Many times you will discover that most investments within a sector or industry rise and fall together which can reduce the effect of diversification.

In addition to creating diversification and having lower fees/expenses, ETFs have a unique attribute that mutual funds do not carry. Recall from the previous section that mutual funds are required to pay capital gains to shareholders at the end of the year. ETFs have no such requirement meaning that any capital gains are simply credited to the value of the fund.

OTHER TYPES OF INVESTMENTS

There are many other investments available in addition to the ones discussed above. However, most of these 'alternative' investments are beyond the scope of 'The Family Investor'. Having said that, I still feel it is beneficial to briefly describe some of them to give you an idea of how they work.

Closed-End Funds. A closed-end fund is an investment fund that issues a FIXED number of shares in an actively-managed portfolio of securities. The shares are traded in the market just like stocks, but because closed-end funds represent a portfolio of securities they are very similar to a mutual fund. Attributes of closed-end funds include:

- They may focus on one region or industry

- They invest in stocks, bonds and other securities to gain diversification
- There are several hundred closed-end funds traded on U.S. stock markets
- Fixed interest payments are taxed at the same rate as the investor's income tax rate
- Some closed-end funds are highly leveraged

Hedge Funds. A hedge fund has some similarities to a mutual fund. However, the investment strategies available to hedge funds and the types of investment positions they can take can be very complicated. Understanding the objectives of the hedge fund is very important:

- Hedge funds seek to maximize returns by using aggressive strategies
- They have MUCH higher fees than mutual funds-they can be as much as 20% or even more!
- Investors should consider liquidity limitations as these products often require investors to keep their money in the fund for at least one or more years

Options. An option is a legal contract that gives the buyer of the option the *right*, but not the obligation, to buy or sell an investment at a specific price on or before a certain date. The 2 main types of options are *Calls* and *Puts*.

A Call option gives the owner the right, but not the obligation, to BUY a specified amount of an investment at a specified price within a specified time. The specified price is known as the *strike price*. The cost for the right to buy the asset is known as the *premium*. The *expiration date* is the future date, usually every Friday, in which the right to buy the asset expires.

A Put option gives the owner the right, but not the obligation, to SELL a specified amount of an investment at a specified price within a specified time. The specified price is known as the strike price. The cost for the right to sell the asset is known as the premium. The expiration date is the future date, usually every Friday, in which the right to sell the asset expires.

Please remember that options strategies are complex and can carry a great degree of risk including a loss of principal.

T.I.P.S. (TREASURY INFLATION-PROTECTED SECURITIES). United States Treasury inflation-protected securities (TIPS) are fixed-income investments that help provide a hedge (or protection) against inflation risk. They are AAA rated bonds that provide us with what is called a *real rate of return*. The real rate of return of an investment is simply the rate of return of our investment minus the inflation rate. For example, if a mutual fund rose 8% in the year, but inflation that year was 5%, we really only made 3%. TIPS help manage this inflation risk by providing the following:

- Protection against the value of TIPS by adjusting the value upward based on the inflation rate
- Providing interest payments that will increase when TIPS prices rise

FUTURES INVESTING. Futures are contracts on commodities, currencies, and stock market indexes that you buy or sell. When investing in futures you are trying to predict the prices of assets at some point in the future. When a futures investor exercises the right to buy an asset at a specific price, the investor on the other side of the contract is obligated to deliver the goods. This could be oil, currencies, orange juice, pork bellies, and other types of assets. For example, someone buying one October Orange Juice contract at $4 a pound is obligated to accept delivery of 100 pounds of orange juice during the month of October at $4 a pound. If you are a seller of the contract, you are obligated to deliver the orange juice to the buyer. Of course, most of us would never buy or deliver that much orange juice. Futures investors will close out the contract just before it expires.

REITS (REAL ESTATE INVESTMENT TRUSTS). A real estate investment trust (REIT) is a real estate company that offers common shares to investors in an effort to raise capital. The company looks to raise enough capital to then invest in various types of real estate and collect lease payments. A REIT is similar to a stock, which represents ownership in a company. However, a REIT has two interesting features:

- Its main business is managing groups of income-producing real-estate properties
- It is required to distribute most of its profits as dividends to shareholders

To qualify as a REIT with the IRS, a real estate company must pay at least 90% of its taxable profit to investors in the form of dividends. When a company qualifies as a REIT, it is not required to pay corporate income tax. A regular corporation makes a profit and pays corporate taxes. The company then decides what to do with their net profit. They can reinvest their profits, pay out some of the profits to shareholders in the form of dividends, or even keep some of their profits in cash. A REIT simply distributes all or most of its profits to shareholders which allows it to be exempt from most taxes.

Keep in mind that although you may never put your money into these unique investments, it is a good idea to become a more knowledgeable investor. You can decide for yourself if alternative investments will have a place in your portfolio. However, please do not purchase any alternative investments without gaining a full understanding of the risks involved. Managing a simulated portfolio in order to practice for a year or two is a great way to avoid costly mistakes and gain valuable experience.

Key Points to Remember from Chapter 5

- Stocks are riskier investments, but can help you grow your investment portfolio over the long-term
- Bonds are historically safer than stocks and provide more stability
- Interest from municipal bonds is free from federal income taxes
- Mutual funds provide diversification, but can be more expensive to own
- Index funds are less expensive and are a good alternative to actively-managed funds
- It may be a good idea to reinvest dividends and capital gains to accumulate more shares
- Alternative investments are only for experienced investors and should be used with caution

CHAPTER SIX

RETIREMENT ACCOUNTS AND THE IMPORTANCE OF EARLY INVESTING

The longer you wait to start investing, the longer you will likely have to work. However, most of us procrastinate saving for retirement for various reasons including:

- We have too many financial obligations at the present time
- A few years later, we still have too many financial obligations
- We do not want to face reality
- Ten years later, we still do not want to face reality
- We are swimming in debt
- We do not understand the concept of investing
- We do not accept the responsibility of having enough money for retirement
- We are living in a dream world, expecting social security to pay for their retirement

While I certainly understand that people have numerous financial obligations, I do not accept that as an excuse to put off saving and investing for the long-term for a comfortable retirement. That may sound abrasive to some people, but that is okay. I am not one to sugar-coat anything. It is our responsibility to have enough money saved up over the years to live the retirement lifestyle we always dreamed about. It is not the responsibility of the government, your employer, or even your children to take care of you when you retire. By the way, social security was created to simply keep people above the poverty level. However, like anything else, when you start giving people entitlements, they begin to exaggerate their expectations. Social security was not created to provide you with your dream retirement. Furthermore, your social security benefits in retirement will likely only cover your basic necessities. Even that may be a stretch! Okay, enough of my preaching! In this chapter we will talk about the importance of early investing as well as the types of retirement accounts that are available to us as investors including the advantages of each.

THE BENEFITS OF EARLY INVESTING

Compounding is when your earnings from your savings and investments create additional earnings. In other words, compounding is when your earnings generate earnings. The more earnings you create and keep working for you, the more earnings you make. As a matter of fact, compounding makes your money grow exponentially!

For compounding to work it requires two items; time and the reinvestment of earnings. When you are young, time is on your side. The longer you have to invest (or the younger you are), the more time you have for compounding to do its job. Table 6.1 on the following page reveals striking results. If you invested $3,000 per year at an average annual return of 6% starting at age 20, you could grow your investments to approximately $676,000 by age 65. However, look what happens if you delayed investing for retirement until age 35. Keeping the same assumptions, you could have about $251,000 by age 65. Consequently, if you wait until you are 45 years old, you may only be able to grow your money to about $117,000 by age 65. Yes, I know you may be thinking to yourself, "I will have more money to invest when I am 35 or 45 because I will be making more money." You are correct in thinking that you will be making more money when you are in your prime working years. However, you will also have more expenses to consider such as upcoming college expenses for your children. Trust me when I tell you that life can throw you many curve balls and can get very costly as time goes on. The most important concept to grasp from Table 6.1 is the power of time and the significant effect it has on your future nest egg. In other words, start investing now! Stop making excuses and begin saving and investing tomorrow!

Table 6.1

AGE to BEGIN INVESTING	AMOUNT at AGE 65
20	$676,524
25	$492,143
30	$354,363
35	$251,405
40	$174,469
45	$116,978
50	$74,018

$3,000 annual investment at 6% annual growth, assuming reinvestment of all earnings and no tax

The second component of compounding is the reinvestment of earnings. This means that if you invest the earnings you made from your investments, you will generate additional money on those earnings. The alternative would be to take your earnings and spend it. Obviously, that would not be a smart decision. For example, let's assume you invest $2,000 just one time into ABC stock that pays a 5% annual dividend. Let's also assume that ABC's stock price goes up an average of 8% per year and the company raises its dividend about 8% per year. Now, before we go any further, I need to stress that there are no stocks out there that are going to go up exactly 8% per year. Nor will any company increase their annual dividend exactly 8% per year. Realistically, stocks will go up some years (possibly more than 8%) and certainly will go down some years. Additionally, some companies might reduce their annual dividend or even get rid of it. There are no guarantees. This example is purely hypothetical to understand the negative effects of not reinvesting your stock dividends or any other earnings you generate from your investments. Anyway, using our assumptions, you may have about $235,000 after 40 years if you reinvested all of the dividends! And if you did NOT reinvest the dividends, you might only have about $42,000 after 40 years. $42,000 is definitely still a good amount, but I think you can see the significant difference when choosing to reinvest all of your earnings from your investments.

HOW DO I CHOOSE AN APPROPRIATE INVESTMENT ACCOUNT?

Many young couples and families have already begun to invest in their company retirement plans or in an account at an investment firm. For those of you who have started, congratulations! You are on your way to financial independence. If you have been procrastinating, you should start as soon as possible. Either way, it is important to understand the various types of investment and retirement accounts that are available. In this chapter, we will discuss the main types of accounts that you will likely be able to open. Keep in mind that an investment account is simply used to hold your investments. Each type of account, however, may have unique advantages. Many people ask me about the rate of return they can expect when opening up a particular investment account. My reply is always to remind them that their rate of return is not dependent on the account, but dependent on the investments you choose to buy within the account. The account itself may have some tax advantages, which we will talk about shortly, but your account value only grows as much as your investments within the account grow.

STANDARD BROKERAGE ACCOUNT

Your 28 years old and recently married. After reading the stimulating information in 'The Family Investor', you have decided to invest your money! Your father-in-law gives you the phone number for his financial advisor. Timidly, you make the phone call and proceed to talk to the financial advisor about investing your money. He explains to you that you need to open a brokerage account and make a cash deposit before you can actually purchase an investment. Later that day you visit his office, fill out and sign all the necessary paperwork, and hand him a check for $10,000 that will be deposited in your new investment account. Finally, he recommends that you purchase a balanced mutual fund with your money. Feeling overwhelmed with the entire process, you nod in agreement and realize that you would have agreed to any investment the financial advisor recommended!

In the scenario above, you opened up a standard brokerage account, also known as a cash account. This is the most basic type of investment account that is available to you. You open the account, deposit cash, and buy investments. You will be able to view your statements and track your investments online. If your investment pays dividends, interest, or capital gains you will receive these earnings as cash that will be credited to your account. Of course, what do you think would be the smart thing to do with the earnings? Hopefully, you realize the smart thing to do would be to reinvest any earnings into more shares of your investments. Keep in mind, however, that any earnings you generate from your investments in a standard brokerage account can trigger a taxable event.

401K PLAN

A 401k plan is a type of retirement account established by your employer for the benefit of you, the employee. By the way, 401k does not stand for $401,000. 401k is just line 401/Section k on the tax code in the United States. The 401k plan is considered a *qualified plan* and is required to adhere to *ERISA* standards set by federal law. ERISA stands for the Employee Retirement Income Security Act and is the law which private industries must follow in order to protect their employees. The 401k plan is also considered a *defined-contribution plan*. In a defined contribution plan, you make contributions to the plan and decide which investments you will purchase. You usually can only invest in mutual funds within your 401k and can choose them from a list provided by the investment firm who sponsors the plan. Additionally, there is a maximum amount each year you are allowed to contribute into your plan. The maximum contribution amount for the current year can be found on the irs.gov website. There are three main advantages of participating in a 401k plan:

- You make contributions on a *pre-tax basis*
- Your investment earnings grow *tax-deferred*
- Employers usually provide matching contributions to your account (FREE MONEY!!)

Table 6.2 below shows the significant tax savings from simply contributing on a pre-tax basis to your 401k plan. In the table, you will see that contributing $10,000 in one year will save you $2,000 if you pay 20% in federal income taxes. Notice the significant difference in the amount of taxes you are paying when you choose to NOT take advantage of contributing to a 401k plan. In this case you are making a 20% return on your money because that is how much you do not have to pay in income taxes. This is because you reduced your taxable income by contributing $10,000 to your 401k plan. Ask yourself this question; can you find an investment that returns 20% to you instantly? I don't think so! And now we have $6,000 that can be invested in various mutual funds that will provide us with earnings and will likely rise in value over the long-term. Furthermore, any earnings from dividends, interest, and capital gains are *tax-deferred*. This means that you will not have to pay any taxes on your earnings as your investments grow in value, unlike the earnings you generate in a standard brokerage account.

Table 6.2

CONTRIBUTE TO 401k		DO NOT CONTRIBUTE TO 401k	
Gross Salary	$50,000	Gross Salary	$50,000
401k Contributions	$6,000	401k Contributions	$0
Taxable Income	$44,000	Taxable Income	$50,000
Income Tax Rate	20%	Income Tax Rate	20%
Income Tax Paid	$8,800	Income Tax Paid	$10,000

Aside from saving money on taxes, most employers will provide a matching contribution to your 401k plan. I find it shocking that many people do not contribute enough into their 401k to get the full company match. That is money left on the table. Please make sure you do not make this mistake. If necessary, call the 401k plan sponsor to find out how much money you need to contribute to get the full matching amount. Table 6.3 on the following page shows a typical employer match when contributing just $6,000 to your 401k plan. Just for contributing $6,000 to the plan, you are receiving $1,500 in matching contributions which is a 25% instant return on your investment! Furthermore, you can invest that $1,500 in mutual funds which will hopefully grow over time.

Table 6.3

CONTRIBUTE TO 401k		DO NOT CONTRIBUTE TO 401k	
Gross Salary	$50,000	Gross Salary	$50,000
401k Contributions	$6,000	401k Contributions	$0
Employer Match	$1,500	Employer Match	$0
Total Contributions	$7,500	Total Contributions	$0
$1,500 in FREE MONEY that you can invest!!			

There is one caveat to matching contributions. You often only have the right to keep the matching contributions after working a specific length of time for your employer. In other words, any matching contributions your employer makes on your behalf will not be available to you unless you are vested. *Vesting* is the process by which you earn the right to keep the matching contributions. It is possible to be fully vested for matching contributions immediately, though it may be less common. Make sure if you leave your employer for any reason, you understand how much of the matching contributions are vested. Below are a couple of key points about vested matching contributions:

- You are ALWAYS 100% vested in your own contributions to your 401k
- You are usually 100% vested in the matching contributions after 3 or more years, but typically 5 years

ESOP (EMPLOYEE STOCK OWNERSHIP PLAN)

An Employee Stock Ownership Plan (ESOP) is a defined contribution plan offered by many large publicly-traded companies by which the investment is in the company stock. The main advantage of an ESOP is that you can purchase your company's stock at a discount, usually about 15%. For example, if the price of the stock is at $60 per share at the time you purchase it, you will only have to pay $51 per share ($60 X (1 - 15%)). However, you cannot simultaneously sell the stock after it is purchased and cash in on your instant 15% profit. Much like matching contributions, you can only sell the stock after a specific period of time. ESOPs usually have their own vesting schedule independent from an employer matching contribution schedule.

Keep in mind, since you are only invested in your company's stock in an ESOP, your risk is significantly greater. I have witnessed a few acquaintances of mine who lost a significant amount of their retirement savings by only participating in their ESOP. If you need more proof of how risky owning just one stock can be, look up the story of Enron on the Internet. There is nothing wrong with participating in an ESOP, however, it is a good idea to keep it to a minimum. You can choose to contribute to both an ESOP and a 401k plan at the same time which could be a good strategy to use that allows you to take advantage of the discount on your company stock as well as being well-diversified in your overall retirement portfolio.

HEALTH SAVINGS ACCOUNT (HSA)

A health savings account (HSA) is a tax-advantaged way to save for certain medical expenses now and in the future. Many large employers will offer this type of plan to its employees, but any individual can establish one outside of his or her employer. To be eligible to contribute to an HSA, you need to get a certain kind of health plan called a High Deductible Health Plan (or HDHP). An HDHP is basically a high deductible, low premium health insurance plan. HSAs have a maximum annual contribution limit which can be found on the irs.gov website. Benefits of a health savings include:

- Many HSAs offer investment options, such as mutual funds
- Just like an IRA, contributions to the HSA may be tax-deductible for an individual
- Contributions to the HSA are pre-tax if established through your employer
- Withdrawals to pay for qualified medical expenses are never taxed, even before age 59 ½
- Investment earnings grow on a tax-deferred basis if withdrawn for non-qualified medical expenses
- Your HSA contributions do not count toward your taxable income for federal taxes
- Your HSA contributions do not count toward your taxable income for most state taxes
- Any unused funds carry over from year to year

Qualified medical expenses are fairly extensive and include dental and vision costs. For a complete list of eligible medical expenses, visit the hsacenter.com website. Be careful when withdrawing the funds for non-qualified medical expenses because you will be taxed at your income-tax rate, plus 20% if you're under 65. As always, tax laws change, so make sure you keep up to date with contribution and distribution rules.

403(b) & 457 PLANS

403(b) and 457 plans are very similar to 401(k) plans. They have the same contribution limits, they allow pre-tax contributions, and they must meet specific requirements to withdraw money from the plan. However, there are some slight differences including:

- 403(b) and 457 plans are offered by nonprofit organizations and government employers while 401(k) plans are offered by for-profit companies
- 403(b) plans are not required to follow ERISA regulations while *most* 457 plans are not required to follow ERISA regulations
- Most 403(b) plans do not offer employer matching contributions, but many 457 plans do, although not nearly as much as companies that offer 401(k) plans
- 403(b) and 457 plans allow multiple providers to administer the plans, including insurance and investment firms

Examples of institutions that commonly offer 403(b) and 457 plans include public schools, colleges, universities, charities, state and local governments, and other tax-exempt entities. The significant difference between 403(b) plans and 457 plans involves rules pertaining to withdrawing money from the plan, also known as taking a *distribution*. We will discuss distribution rules for retirement accounts at the end of this chapter. It is also important to note that some people may be able to contribute to *both* a 403(b) and 457 plan, essentially doubling the amount you can contribute when compared to a 401(k) plan.

SEP (SIMPLIFIED EMPLOYEE PENSION)

A Simplified Employee Pension (or SEP) is a type of retirement account that is suitable for many of us who are self-employed and do not have access to a 401k plan. Also, many smaller companies offer their employees access to a SEP because they are not big enough to make it feasible to implement a 401k plan. A SEP, much like a 401k, will allow you to participate in tax-advantaged retirement planning, but is not considered a qualified plan. Below are the main advantages of participating in a SEP:

- Contributions to a SEP are tax-deductible, therefore contributions are ultimately not taxed
- Your investment earnings grow on a tax-deferred basis, just like in a 401k
- Contribution limits can be significantly higher than a 401k plan
- You can invest in a wide variety of investments

Since contributions to a SEP are tax-deductible, the only difference between a SEP and a 401k is *when* you realize the tax savings. In a 401k, you realize the tax savings instantly when making a contribution. In a SEP, you have to wait until you file your tax return for that year. However, contribution limits for a SEP can be considerably higher when compared to a 401k. Basically, you can contribute up to 25% of your MAGI (Modified Adjusted Gross Income), but with a maximum amount. For example, if your company has a SEP plan and your MAGI for the year is $100,000, the company can contribute up to $25,000 in your SEP for the year. If you are self-employed and make $100,000 for the year, your maximum contribution will be less than $25,000. Visit the irs.gov website to determine the maximum contribution to a SEP for self-employed individuals, the maximum contribution amount for the current year for a SEP, as well as the definition of MAGI.

One of the greatest benefits of a SEP is the different types of investments you can purchase within your account. Unlike 401k plans, which usually only allow you to invest in mutual funds, SEPs allow you to invest in individual stocks, bonds, certificates of deposits, mutual funds, certain commodities, and more. This gives you greater flexibility when constructing an investment portfolio and planning for retirement.

You can see how SEPs can be a great type of retirement plan for self-employed individuals. I come across many electricians, plumbers, contractors, consultants, and others who do not realize they can establish and contribute to a SEP plan even though they work for themselves. Many of us are already self-employed or will become self-employed in our lifetime. It is good to know that this type of retirement plan is available to us if needed.

TRADITIONAL IRA

A *Traditional IRA* (IRA stands for Individual Retirement Arrangement, but we usually just call it an Individual Retirement Account) is a retirement account by which you can establish and contribute money into, **in addition to,** a retirement plan from your employer. Below are some advantages of a Traditional IRA:

- Contributions to a Traditional IRA *may* be tax-deductible
- Your investment earnings grow on a tax-deferred basis, just like in a 401k and SEP
- You can invest in a wide variety of investments

Just like qualified plans and SEPs, you may not have to pay any tax on contributions. Notice how you *MAY* not have to pay taxes on your contributions. If you make too much money you will not be allowed to deduct your contributions from your income. There is also a maximum contribution limit for any given year for the Traditional IRA. Again, check the irs.gov website for income and contribution limits.

Much like the 401k and SEP, earnings generated from your investments within your Traditional IRA are tax-deferred. Another nice feature of a Traditional IRA is that you can establish and contribute to one on behalf of your spouse even if he or she does not have any taxable compensation for the year. This allows you to essentially double the amount of money you can invest for retirement. Remember that an IRA is for an individual so your spouse's Traditional IRA will be a completely separate account under his or her name. Additionally, just like a SEP, you can invest in individual stocks, bonds, certificates of deposits, mutual funds, certain commodities, and more.

ROTH IRA

Generally speaking, any money you earn from your investments are taxed. That's right!! Uncle Sam takes his share of the money you make from your investment portfolio. When it comes to most retirement plans, however, there are significant differences on *when* you are taxed. Most retirement plans are designed so that any contributions (money you put into the plan) are either tax-deductible or pre-tax, and distributions (money you take out of the plan) are taxed based on your income tax rate at the time. Essentially, this just means you are NOT taxed on your contributions, but you ARE taxed on your distributions. Therefore, if you had a choice, would you rather be taxed on your contributions to your retirement plan or on your distributions? More specifically, given your current taxable income level, when would you prefer to be taxed in your retirement plans? This is a very interesting question that could shed some light about which type of IRA would be appropriate for you from a tax perspective. Think about the answer in terms of your situation as an investor. In other words, are you paying little right now in federal income taxes or are you in a high income tax bracket? To answer this question, we need to take a look at the *Roth IRA*. A Roth IRA is a retirement account where contributions are **NEVER** tax-deductible, earnings grow on a **tax-free** basis, and qualified distributions are **ALWAYS** tax free. From a tax perspective, it is the polar opposite of the retirement plans we have already talked about. In a Roth IRA, you make *after-tax* contributions, meaning you do not save money on taxes upfront. Instead, you save money on taxes when you take money out of your Roth IRA. The Roth IRA is, however, similar to the Traditional IRA in that the maximum contribution limits are the same as well as having the ability to purchase a wide variety of investments.

Examples of Investing Within a Roth IRA

- Lisa, age 68, takes a $3,000 distribution from her Roth IRA. Her federal income tax rate is 35%. How much will she be taxed on the distribution? The answer is zero! She will not be taxed at all since the distribution was from a Roth IRA and she is over 59 ½ (see *Distribution Rules* in the following section).
- Matt, age 30, will make around $10,000 this year working part-time. He decides to open up a Roth IRA and contribute $4,000 into it. He decides to buy $4,000 worth of mutual funds within the account.
- Denise, age 26, already contributes enough into her 401k retirement plan through her employer to receive the full amount of matching contributions. She is only in the 15% federal tax bracket. Denise then decides to contribute additional funds in her Roth IRA.

I'd like to shed some light on determining which IRA (Traditional or Roth) you should contribute to. While there is never one answer that fits everyone's situation, you should probably invest in a Roth IRA if your *marginal tax rate* is low. Your marginal tax rate is basically the highest rate of federal income tax that you pay. For example, if your marginal tax rate is only 15%, it may be wise to contribute to a Roth IRA and pay the 15% in taxes right away, but pay none when you take a qualified distribution in retirement. While we do not have a crystal ball to foresee income tax rates in the future, it would be difficult to believe that tax rates will *not* rise in the years ahead. Unless we see major changes in government entitlement programs like Social Security, Medicare, and Medicaid, the government will have to raise taxes in order to keep these programs alive.

Finally, there are two other types of retirement accounts related to the Roth IRA that have become popular in recent years. The Roth 401(k) or Roth 403(b) combines the tax benefits of a Roth IRA and the higher contribution limits allowed in 401(k) and 403(b) plans. Again, it is a personal decision whether to pay taxes now or later and is based on many factors. Please consult a tax advisor for professional advice on whether or not a Roth 401(k) or Roth 403(b) is right for you.

DISTRIBUTIONS FROM RETIREMENT PLANS

Distributions are simply defined as the removal of assets from a retirement account. In other words, it is when you withdrawal money from your account. The significance of a distribution is the fact that you have to pay taxes on the amount you withdrawal in most of the retirement plans we have discussed. The major distribution rules include, but are not limited to:

- In general, distributions, or withdrawals, from a retirement plan must occur after age 59 ½

- In general, distributions that occur before 59 ½ will be charged a 10% early distribution penalty
- There are some exceptions to the 10% penalty rule
- Retirement Plan Owners are required to pay income taxes when receiving a distribution. The exception is the Roth IRA, Roth 401(k), and Roth 403(b), where distributions are TAX-FREE
- Retirement Plan Owners must begin required minimum distributions (RMDs) the year he or she reaches age 73. The exception is the Roth IRA, where there is no required minimum distribution
- Roth 401(k) and Roth 403(b) owners also are not NOT required to take minimum distributions at 73 just like regular Roth IRA owners

Notice the 10% penalty rule if you take a distribution before age 59 ½. The reason why you will be penalized 10% is because the government wants to create an incentive for you to save for your retirement years. However, you will not be penalized if you take a distribution before age 59 ½ for the following reasons:

- Upon and after death of the account owner
- If the account owner becomes disabled
- If the account owner is at least 55 and has left his employer
- For certain medical expenses
- For higher education expenses
- For a down payment on a 1st home

One quick note regarding 457 plan distributions. Anyone still working at the employer that sponsors their 457 plan cannot take distributions until age 73 without penalty. However, if the employee leaves that employer, the employee can take distributions at any age without penalty. This is unique to 457 plans when compared to the other retirement plans we talked about.

Key Points to Remember from Chapter 6

- Start investing now!!
- Reinvest ALL of the earnings you generate from your investments
- Contribute enough to your 401k plan to receive the full company match
- If self-employed, take advantage of a SEP
- Consider a Roth IRA if you do not want your distributions to be taxed
- Generally speaking, do not withdraw money from your retirement plan until you are 59 ½

CHAPTER SEVEN

EDUCATION PLANNING: DO NOT SACRIFICE YOUR RETIREMENT!!

It is no secret that higher education expenses have far outweighed inflation over the years. Private school costs have risen to ridiculous levels. Even the costs associated with a standard four-year degree from a public university could very well be in the six-figure range. While this trend *may* slow down over time, it is especially important to plan early for these overwhelming costs. The most important thing to remember is to make sure your retirement plan remains on track. In other words, do NOT use your retirement assets to pay for your child's education expenses. Unfortunately, that is what many families decide to do when they realize that they did not save and invest enough money to pay for all education-related costs. I have met many people who fall into this category and can honestly say that most of them regret using their retirement money to pay for college expenses. Some of them are finding it extremely difficult to make ends meet and also have to maintain a job well into their retirement years to pay for basic necessities.

While I am not writing this book for the purpose of preaching, I do feel the need to express my opinion regarding whose responsibility it is to pay for higher education. I believe that it is the responsibility of one's *entire* family to make sure that each young person receives the education they deserve. This means that parents AND students should have ownership in the related expenses. It is certainly understandable, given the incredibly high costs of college, if you do not agree with me, and that is fine. I am simply trying to get the point across regarding paying for college in a responsible manner. It is okay if your child has to pay for a portion of the expenses. Quite frankly, I feel that it can be an important lesson on how to appreciate the value of a dollar and to not take things for granted. Many college graduates are successful in their careers, but have nothing to show for it because they never had to 'suffer' from a financial perspective. This does not mean letting your children go hungry or allow them to live on the streets! It simply means that they need to understand the concept of sacrifice. If they have to pay for some of their expenses, maybe they will not be able to buy unnecessary items on a consistent basis because they will be forced to save money to help pay for their degree. Many people from my generation had to pay for college. Yes, I understand that it is much more expensive now, but paying for your own college degree is a lifelong lesson that teaches you how to be financially responsible and can be invaluable in your quest for wealth. Conversely, I still remember some of my friends receiving a significant amount of money every month from their parents for 'entertainment' even though their parents were paying their entire cost of college. Obviously, that means blowing the money on things many of us remember from our college experience! How can anyone learn anything about financial responsibility if they have always had everything paid for them? How about suggesting to your child that he or she get a job to pay for all of his or her 'entertainment' expenses?! Anyway, while you may or may not agree with me, I hope you can respect my point of view. There are also people who feel that if they save for college, their child's eligibility status for financial aid will be significantly reduced. This is not necessarily true. Besides, similar to your retirement, it is not the responsibility of the government or any institution to pay for education expenses. Expecting someone else to pay for these expenses is like gambling. Things in life continuously change and there is no guarantee that the cost of your child's college degree will be paid for by someone else. Accept the responsibility as a parent and/or a student and do the right thing by planning early!

In this chapter, we will learn about the various ways in which you can begin saving and investing for education expenses. We will discuss the following education planning topics in detail:

- Coverdell Education Savings Account (ESA)
- 529 Plans (Including Pre-Paid Tuition Programs)
- Free Application for Federal Student Aid (FAFSA) and Financial Aid Eligibility
- Types of Student Loans
- Education Tax Credits
- Useful Websites for Education Planning

COVERDELL EDUCATION SAVINGS ACCOUNT (ESA)

The Coverdell Education Savings Account (ESA) allows individuals to deposit and invest money in an educational savings account for an eligible beneficiary. Some of the most important features of an ESA include the following:

- Much like an IRA, you can purchase a variety of investments within an ESA
- All earnings from the investments within an ESA grow on a tax-free basis
- The money can be withdrawn tax-free when used for qualified educational expenses

- The beneficiary must use the funds before the age of 30 for qualified educational expenses
- The account must be started and all contributions made before the child is 18.
- You can use the money within an ESA for college AND pre-college private school expenses

Although there are limitations on how much you can contribute annually to an ESA, it is an incredibly flexible account when considering that you can invest in individual stocks and bonds, mutual funds, CDs, and more. This allows you to construct an appropriate investment portfolio to help you reach your education planning goals. I will tell you, however, that the annual contribution limit is very low when compared to other education planning vehicles such as the 529 plan, which we will talk about next. As of this writing, the annual contribution limit to an ESA was just $2,000. There are also income limits, although rather high, that may prevent you from contributing in any given year. These income limits as well as updated annual contribution limits to an ESA can be found on the irs.gov website.

Much like the incredible Roth IRA, earnings within an ESA grow on a tax-free basis! Recall that earnings grown on a tax-free basis is different than earnings grown on a tax-deferred basis. Tax-deferred means that you are paying the taxes later. More specifically, you are paying taxes when you take a withdrawal (distribution). In an ESA, earnings grow on a tax-*free* basis which means you will not have to pay any taxes on any earnings when taking a distribution as long as the money is used for qualified education expenses. Qualified education expenses include:

- Tuition and Fees
- Books, Supplies, & Equipment

- Special Needs Services
- Room and Board
- School-Provided Transportation
- School Uniforms
- Computers & Internet Usage

For example, suppose you contribute a total of $10,000 over five years into an ESA and the investments within the account have earned about $1,500. You already paid income taxes on the $10,000 through your paycheck. The beneficiary (or the child) of the ESA will not have to pay taxes on the $1,500 earned if used for qualified education expenses, unlike a standard brokerage account that we discussed in Chapter 6. Notice how I stated that the *beneficiary* will not have to pay taxes on the $1,500 earned. A beneficiary is someone who receives distributions from certain types of accounts or even a life insurance policy whereas the account owner is the person making the contributions to an account. In an ESA, it is the beneficiary's responsibility to pay ALL taxes and penalties on any *non-qualified* distributions. Essentially, non-qualified distributions refer to any money withdrawn from an ESA that is not used for education-related expenses. If the beneficiary withdraws money for non-qualified education expenses, there is a 10% penalty tax AND your child will have to pay income tax on the earnings. Let's take a look at some other ESA distribution examples:

Katie, age 19, takes a $15,000 distribution from her ESA to pay for her college tuition. Her income tax rate is 15%. Will she be taxed on the distribution?

In the example above, Katie will not incur any income taxes on the $15,000 distribution from her ESA because she is using the money to pay for her college tuition.

Richard, age 18 and a student at a local private high school, takes a $500 distribution from his ESA to pay for new school uniforms. His income tax rate is 10%. Will he be taxed on the distribution?

Once again, the beneficiary, Richard, will not incur any income taxes on his distribution from the ESA because he is using the money for new school uniforms which is a qualified education expense. Notice how Richard attends a local private high school. Another benefit of an ESA is that the money can be used for higher education expenses as well as private school expenses prior to college.

Mike, age 20 takes a $4,000 distribution from his ESA to pay for a sound system for his awesome new rock band. His income tax rate is 15%. Will he be taxed on the distribution?

A new sound system for Mike's rock band! That *sounds* incredibly exciting (pun intended), except that Mike will now have to pay income taxes on any earnings PLUS an additional 10%.

Monica turned 30 years old about two weeks ago. She proceeds to take an $18,000 distribution from her ESA to pay for her college tuition costs. Her income tax rate is 25%. Will she be taxed on the distribution?

Unfortunately for Monica, she will have to pay income taxes on any earnings as well as an additional 10% penalty. Monica should have taken a full distribution before she reached age 30 because taking all distributions by age 30 is one of the requirements of maintaining the tax benefits of an ESA.

In some ESA distribution cases, the 10% penalty rule does not apply. These are known as the 10% penalty rule exceptions. Here are a few examples of exceptions to the 10% penalty rule for ESAs:

- Any withdrawals made due to the beneficiary's death or disability
- Any adjustments made to qualified expenses due to education tax credits (discussed later in this chapter)
- Any withdrawals made up to the amount the beneficiary receives in tax-free scholarships

As an ESA account owner, usually a parent or grandparent, you can change the beneficiary of the ESA at any time or rollover the funds into an ESA of a family member of the previous beneficiary. This can be useful if the current beneficiary does not plan on attending college. Worst case scenario is that none of your children go to college in which case you can simply take a full distribution, but pay taxes and penalties. Keep in mind, your investments within the account likely grew over time so you still made money!

One final note regarding ESAs and the impact it has on financial aid eligibility. The value of an ESA is treated as an asset of the account owner (again, usually the parent) which has a low impact on financial aid eligibility. However, if the account owner happens to be the student, the impact on financial aid eligibility is much greater. That is why it is usually smarter to have a parent as an ESA account owner.

529 PLANS

529 plans were created under the Small Business Job Protection Act of 1996 as a way of allowing taxpayers to save for higher education expenses for a designated beneficiary. The "529" part of the name is just section 529 of the IRS tax code. The 529 Plan allows individuals to deposit and invest money in an educational savings account for an eligible beneficiary. Every state in the United States has at least one type of 529 plan. Although many of us are already

familiar with the advantages of a 529 plan and may already be contributing to one, there are many interesting characteristics that many people may not be familiar with. Some of the most important features of a 529 plan include:

- Like the education savings account (ESA), earnings in a 529 plan accumulate on a tax-free basis
- Like the ESA, money can be withdrawn tax-free when used for qualified educational expenses
- The contribution limits for a 529 plan are considerably higher than those for an ESA
- Contributions can be made for each designated beneficiary without incurring federal gift taxes
- Like the ESA, you can use the money from a 529 plan for higher-education expenses AND pre-college private school expenses
- Investments are typically limited to mutual funds and cash investments such as CDs

(Note: Investors should consider the investment objectives, risks, charges, and expenses associated with 529 plans before investing. More information about 529 plans is available in each issuer's official statement, which should be read carefully before investing. Also, before investing, consider whether your state offers a 529 plan that provides residents with favorable state tax benefits.)

The maximum amount that may be contributed on behalf of a designated beneficiary varies among states. However, 529 plans were also created as an estate planning tool by allowing account owners to contribute a lump sum that would shelter contributions from their estate. This is why many wealthy grandparents will use a 529 plan to help out their grandchildren. Rather than give their grandchildren money to deposit in their savings accounts, grandparents will open up a 529 plan and contribute a sizable amount in order to protect those assets from estate taxes when they pass on. Furthermore, the beneficiary would not incur a gift tax up to the maximum lump sum amount allowed. Normally, an individual or married couple can give an annual maximum gift amount to any person without that person paying a gift tax. With 529 plans, any individual or married couple can give **FIVE** years of gifting in one lump sum without the recipient paying a gift tax. Keep in mind that if an individual or married couple takes advantage of this special gifting rule for 529 contributions by giving the recipient the maximum amount allowed for five years, they will not be able to give that person any more money for the next five years beyond the 5-year maximum amount without them paying a gift tax. Again, the irs.gov website will list the current maximum gift that individuals and married couples can give a recipient without incurring gift taxes. Let's take a look at an example of contributing a lump sum to a 529 plan.

John and Jane have four grandchildren and have accumulated a large nest egg for their retirement. They are concerned about estate taxes when they pass away and have started to think about estate planning as a way to conserve their wealth for their family. They also would like to help their grandchildren pay for their college expenses. John researches the gifting laws on the irs.gov website and finds that an individual can gift up to $17,000 per year while a married couple can gift up to $34,000 per year without the recipient paying a gift tax. Since John and Jane are married, they decide to contribute $170,000 ($34,000 X 5 years) into a 529 plan for each grandchild. The grandchildren will not be liable for any gift tax, but any subsequent gifts to the grandchildren within the next five years will definitely be subject to taxes.

Similar to the ESA, if the beneficiary withdraws money for non-education expenses, there is a 10% penalty tax AND your child will have to pay income tax on the earnings. Qualifying education expenses again include:

- Tuition and Fees
- Books, Supplies, & Equipment
- Special Needs Services
- Room and Board
- School-Provided Transportation
- School Uniforms
- Computers & Internet Usage

Below are some examples of distributions from a 529 plan:

Jeff, age 19 and a student at Michigan State University, takes a $2,000 distribution from his 529 plan to pay for books. His income tax rate is 10%. Will he be taxed on the distribution?

In the example above, Jeff will not incur any income taxes on the $2,000 distribution from his 529 plan because he is using the money to pay for his books.

Laura, age 20, takes a $10,000 distribution from her 529 plan to pay for a rare painting of SpongeBob Squarepants for her snobbish boyfriend. Her income tax rate is 10%. Will she be taxed on the distribution?

The 529 beneficiary, Laura, will certainly have to pay income taxes on any earnings from her distribution from the 529 because she is using the money for a non-qualified expense. She will also have to pay an additional 10% tax penalty. (Not smart Laura--I think it's time to find a new boyfriend!)

Mark, age 16 and a high school student at Don Bosco Prep, takes an $800 distribution from his 529 Plan to pay for new school uniforms. His income tax rate is 10%. Will he be taxed on the distribution?

Fortunately for Mark, he will not have to pay income taxes on any earnings from the distribution. Mark realizes that qualified distributions from a 529 plan are also for pre-college private school expenses.

Just like the ESA, the 10% penalty rule does not apply in certain cases. Here are a few examples of exceptions to the 10% penalty rule for 529s:

- Any withdrawals made due to the beneficiary's death or disability
- Any adjustments made to qualified expenses due to education tax credits (discussed later in this chapter)
- Any withdrawals made up to the amount the beneficiary receives in tax-free scholarships
- Any withdrawals up to $10,000 to pay back student loans

529 plans basically fall into two categories:

- College Savings Plan
- Pre-Paid Tuition Plan (sometimes referred to as a Guaranteed Savings Plan)

Most state 529 plans offer a *College Savings Plan* which allow contributions to be made and invested in a variety of age-based investment options where the underlying investments become more conservative as the beneficiary gets closer to his or her college years. These investments are generally made in mutual funds and/or a collection of mutual funds. The account owner can make changes to the investment choices if needed, although there may be some limitations on how often changes can be made. In addition, many savings plans offer cash investment options such as certificate of deposits designed to protect an investor's account value.

Savingforcollege.com is one of the best and most informative websites to find specific 529 plan information by state. By the way, you can open up a 529 plan from any state regardless of where you live. However, be aware of certain rules on state income tax deductions, if applicable. Talk to your tax advisor for more information on state tax deductions for 529 plan contributions.

Another little known fact about 529 College Savings Plan is that any non-qualified distributions made from a 529 plan, up to the amount the beneficiary receives in tax-free scholarships, are not penalized. The beneficiary will still have to pay income tax on the earnings portion of the distribution up to the amount of the scholarship, but it will not be subject to the 10% penalty tax. Let's take a look at an example.

Jennifer is the beneficiary of a 529 College Savings Plan with an account value of $100,000 and has just been accepted to a well-known state university. The university has offered her $5,000 per year ($20,000 for 4 years) in scholarship money which brings her out-of-pocket costs for a 4-year degree down to $80,000. Since Jennifer has $100,000 in her 529 plan, but only needs $80,000, she can take the remaining $20,000 out as a non-qualified distribution without being penalized an additional 10%. Once again, this is because she received $20,000 in scholarship money from her school. Keep in mind, however, that the account owner can choose to change the beneficiary to another family member after Jennifer pays the $80,000 in college expenses. In that case, the $20,000 would move into the name of the new beneficiary.

The 529 account owner can also rollover all or a portion of 529 assets into another state plan once every 12 months. However, 529 assets can be rolled over at any time if the beneficiary changes. Please be aware that there may be certain tax implications (positive or negative) when performing a 529 rollover. It is always wise to consult your tax advisor before making any decisions.

As an account owner, you can start a 529 College Savings Plan directly through the state or through a financial advisor. Please be aware that if you access the plan through an advisor, you will be paying more in fees. If you are going to choose an age-based allocation of mutual funds that automatically rebalances as the beneficiary gets older, I see no need to pay the extra fees for having an advisor attached to an account. And remember, this statement is coming from someone who is an experienced financial advisor!

Pre-paid tuition programs are only available in certain states and can be a little more complicated to understand. In general, you purchase tuition credits from the pre-paid tuition state plan which can be used at eligible educational institutions. Essentially you are paying for the cost of college in advance for the designated beneficiary. Advantages of a pre-paid tuition program include:

- Pre-paid tuition programs take the risk of financial markets out of the equation
- You can pay college expenses at eligible colleges and universities at today's prices
- Pre-paid tuition programs usually allow you to use your credits at eligible colleges and universities anywhere in the United States

One of the issues with pre-paid tuition programs is that the cost of the tuition credits vary greatly between community colleges, state schools, state-sponsored schools, and private universities. For example, in Pennsylvania, there is a significant cost difference per credit for Penn State University versus Bloomsburg University. That is because Penn State is a state-*related* university as opposed to simply a state school. Private school costs per credit are even higher. You can look up any state's pre-paid tuition program on the Internet to find out the specific cost per credit for that state. Keep in mind that if your child uses the tuition credits to attend an out-of-state school, there could be significant differences in the value of your credits.

As with an ESA account owner, a 529 plan owner can change the beneficiary of the 529 account at any time. This can be useful if the current beneficiary does not plan on attending college.

FREE APPLICATION FOR FEDERAL STUDENT AID (FAFSA) AND FINANCIAL AID ELIGIBILITY

There is one more note (and an especially important one) regarding 529s and the impact it has on financial aid eligibility. The value of a 529 is treated as an asset of the account owner (again, usually the parent) which has a low impact on financial aid eligibility. As with an ESA, if the account owner happens to be the student, the impact on financial aid eligibility can be much greater. Specifically, 529 plan assets are counted at a maximum rate of 5.64% when calculating the student's *Expected Family Contribution* (or EFC). The EFC is a measure to determine your family's financial situation and to help calculate a student's eligibility for financial aid. If the value of a 529 plan is $50,000 and is owned by the parent, than only $2,820 is counted toward the EFC equation. Always check the fafsa.ed.gov website for current EFC calculation measures.

EFC is an important calculation as part of the *FAFSA* (Free Application for Federal Student Aid) form. The FAFSA form is used by the majority of colleges and universities and helps determine eligibility for financial aid, loans, grants, work-study programs, and much more. *EVERY* student and his or her parents should fill out the FAFSA form. I know what some of you might be thinking right now; "Our income is much too high to receive *any* kind of financial aid." While that *may* be true, it is imperative to understand that many colleges and universities require you to fill out the FAFSA form before receiving any type of scholarship money from the school. You may also be surprised that your child might be eligible for some kind of aid.......so why not try?! You have nothing to lose and everything to gain!

It is especially important to fill out the FAFSA form in a timely manner. Most parents think that they have to wait until they file their tax return before completing the FAFSA. That is not true! It is first come, first serve with the FAFSA form. Parents can estimate their taxes on the form and make adjustments, if needed, after they have filed their tax return. It is much more effective to complete the FAFSA as soon as possible. Below is a short timeline you should follow when filling out the FAFSA form:

1. Approximately 1-2 weeks before October 1st of your child's senior year in high school, go to the fafsa.ed.gov website and apply for a Federal Student Aid (FSA) ID
2. You should receive your FSA ID in about one week or so
3. On October 1st of your child's senior year, go to the fafsa.ed.gov website to complete and submit the form

That's it!! Just get it done as soon as possible. Yes, technically speaking, you usually have until June 30th of your child's senior year of high school to complete and submit the form. However, many parents and students are unaware that every college and university has their own deadline for the FAFSA. It is actually quite comical that the 'federal' deadline is June 30th, but school deadlines are usually earlier. Additionally, some states have their own deadlines for state financial aid. How does that make sense?!

As if it couldn't get more complicated (I really believe they make it complicated on purpose), a small number of schools also require that you submit a *CSS Profile*. A CSS Profile is simply another way for a school to determine financial aid eligibility. It uses different methodologies than the FAFSA and also charges a processing fee that is given to the College Board (how convenient). Just be aware that you only have to complete a CSS Profile if the college or university requests it.

While all of these financial aid rules can be *slightly* overwhelming (can you sense the sarcasm?), you need to understand that things may, and probably will, change over the years. Make sure you work with a trusted tax professional or financial advisor when the time comes to save and invest for higher education. And please beware of individuals who hold themselves out as a 'financial aid specialist' or 'college planning specialist'. Some of them are certainly honest and helpful, but many charge a sizable fee for things that are not difficult to do such as filling out the FAFSA form or simply applying to colleges. And some might recommend inappropriate and expensive types of investments that will provide them large commissions. As a financial advisor, my compliance department will not even allow me to market myself as an education planning specialist or something similar to that. What does that tell you?!

TYPES OF STUDENT LOANS

In a perfect world, our children will graduate college 100% debt-free. However, we all know it is not a perfect world. Therefore, it may be necessary to take out loans to pay for higher education.

Remember, the FAFSA form should be completed in a timely manner to be eligible for any student loan offered by the government.

Before diving into the types of student loans available, I would like to talk about using common sense when your child decides on which college/university to attend. I fully understand that many factors go into the decision-making process when choosing a school, but one of the most important criteria is to NOT have a large amount of debt piled up after he or she graduates. I personally know many young adults that are financially stressed due to overwhelming student loans. Many of them are still living at home because they cannot afford the expenses when living on their own because of their high student loan payments. Never mind the seemingly endless number of college graduates still looking for a job related to their major who are working at low-paying jobs. Yes, I realize that statement does not represent ALL college graduates, but there are more than you may think. As an example, if your son or daughter plans to have a career in education, does it make sense for he or she to attend a $50,000 a year university? I think not!! Of course, if you have the ability to pay the entire college bill for your children without altering your retirement goals, so be it. Most students will not have that luxury afforded to them. Consequently, most students will need to take out loans. Imagine graduating with a teaching degree, attaining a teaching position making the minimum salary for new teachers, and having to make astronomical student loan payments every month. Furthermore, your child will have other expenses to pay such as new clothing for the new job, commuting expenses, maybe a car loan, and much more. And let's not forget about the possibility of living on their own. Highly unlikely in this case, but you never know. It's simple math...*without actual numbers*! If this scenario sounds exaggerated, think again. I personally know teachers who are in this predicament. And please do not think it is confined to just the teaching profession. There are many other careers that do not pay well right out of college that will limit the ability to pay back student loans. Please understand that there is nothing wrong with taking out loans within reason. However, you need to evaluate the cost of a degree relative to the starting salary your child will receive based on his or her profession and, as always, the location of employment. Salary.com is a good website to determine how much someone can make right out of college based on these factors.

There are certainly times when going to a very expensive college might make sense (or cents!!). If your child strives to be a hot-shot attorney or become a politician or even a congressman at some point in his or her career, it definitely helps to attend a well-known Ivy League school or other prestigious institution. There are other careers that fall into this category, but for most people it is just not feasible to pay the high costs unless the college pays for most of it. If your child plans on being an Art major, Nursing major, and in many cases, a Business Management major, is it really wise to be tens of thousands of dollars in debt right out of school? Well, that is what is happening around the country for many college graduates.

Sometimes, choosing an outrageously expensive school is all about "bragging" rights. I find this to be the case more and more. Whether it be the student or the parent, attending a prestigious university seems to make people feel better about themselves by telling everyone around them that they were accepted to a well-known private school. It has become a competition for many of us. As crazy as it sounds, this has become an unfortunate reality. There are numerous state schools in the United States that provide an excellent education for a reasonable price. Many of these schools have excellent reputations and successful job-placement programs as well. And while getting a first significant job out of college *might* be easier when attending an Ivy League school, it is a person's work ethic, problem-solving skills, social skills, and experience that will propel their career advancement.......NOT the name of the school where their degree was earned.

I think I have made my point regarding the relationship between the cost of education and income potential for specific careers. Please remember to be reasonable when choosing a higher educational institution and to not fall into the student loan debt trap. Moving on, the most common types of student loans are:

- Subsidized Stafford Loans
- Unsubsidized Stafford Loans
- Parent PLUS Loans
- Private Loans
- Health Professions Student Loan
- Direct Consolidation Loans

A **Subsidized Stafford Loan** is a low interest rate student loan where the interest is paid by the government until your child graduates. The interest rate is fixed meaning the rate can never go higher. Your child will not have to make payments on the loan until six months after graduation.

An **Unsubsidized Stafford Loan** is a low interest rate student loan which *does* accumulate interest while your child is in school. The interest rate is also fixed for the life of the loan. Again, your

child will not have to make payments on the loan until six months after graduation.

Parent PLUS Loans can have higher fees and higher interest rates, but are fixed for the life of the loan. As the name implies, Parent PLUS Loans are loans that *parents* can take out to help pay for their child's education. This differs from the loans above where it is the student that is responsible for loan payments. However, similar to loans granted to the student, eligibility is determined by the information received on the student's FAFSA form. Parent PLUS loans are unsubsidized. A slight variation of this loan is simply called the **PLUS Loan**. The PLUS Loan is available to graduate students or the parents of graduate students.

Private Student Loans have *variable* interest rates which is much riskier than fixed-rate loans. That is because the interest can, and likely will, change over the years. There is always a chance the rate will go down, but for planning purposes, don't count on it. Private student loans are given based on criteria which assesses the ability to pay back the loan.

A **Health Professions Student Loan** provides low interest rate loans to full-time students to pursue a degree in dentistry, optometry, pharmacy, podiatric medicine, or veterinary medicine. These loans are only given out based on financial need, but can usually be paid back over a longer period of time.

A **Direct Consolidation Loan** combines all of a person's student loans into one loan. This might be a good option for someone who has multiple, high-interest student loans looking for a simple, and potentially less costly way to pay off their debts.

EDUCATION TAX CREDITS

There are basically two education tax credits that reduce your tax liability dollar for dollar. The American Opportunity Credit is a credit up to $2,500 for qualified college educational expenses paid for each student eligible. Expenses include tuition, fees, books and other supplies. The Lifetime Learning Credit is a credit up to $2,000 for qualified college educational expenses paid for each student eligible. Please refer to the irs.gov website for income limitations and/or consult your tax advisor for any changes to these available credits.

USEFUL WEBSITES FOR EDUCATION PLANNING

I have compiled several lists below that will provide you with useful websites to help you in the education planning process. While there are numerous websites for college planning, I have found these to be the most comprehensive. I hope that you will take advantage of the information you find on these sites.

To research colleges:

- bestvalueschools.com
- cappex.com
- collegeboard.org
- colleges.startclass.com
- collegeswimming.com (for students planning on being on their college swim team)
- petersons.com
- princetonreview.com
- thebestschools.org
- unigo.com

To look for scholarships:

- bigfure.collegeboard.org
- cappex.com
- chegg.com
- collegenet.com

- colleges.niche.com
- fastweb.com
- scholarshippoints.com
- scholarships.com
- simpletuition.com
- studentscholarships.org

To learn more about college savings plans:

- collegesavings.org
- finaid.org
- savingforcollege.com
- upromise.com

I am confident you will acknowledge how important it is to plan effectively for higher education expenses. Education planning is obviously one of the cornerstones of building wealth in the overall financial planning process. In the next chapter, we will discover another fundamental aspect of financial planning: how to protect the wealth you have accumulated.

Key Points to Remember from Chapter 7

- It is the parents AND students who should be responsible to pay for higher education expenses
- Do not sacrifice your retirement to pay for your child's education

- Education Savings Plans and 529 Plans are tax-advantaged ways to save for education expenses
- Complete the FAFSA form in a timely manner--**AS SOON AS POSSIBLE!!**
- Choose a school that will not burden you or your child with too much debt

- Become familiar with the different types of student loans available to parents and students

CHAPTER EIGHT

WEALTH PROTECTION AND THE UNDENIABLE NEED FOR INSURANCE

Steve, 45, has a successful career, loving wife, three healthy children, and a four-bedroom, 2 ½ bath home in the suburbs. His life, while certainly challenging, has been an inspiration to many of his childhood and college friends. Steve embraces matrimony and fatherhood and has provided a blissful environment for his family. Even at his place of employment, Steve seems to thrive on a work and social level, creating long-lasting friendships and becoming a leader among his peers.

From a financial perspective, Steve has followed *most* of the information he read from 'The Family Investor', including formulating a budget, staying out of debt, attaining a reasonable mortgage, contributing enough to his 401k plan to get the full company match, and opening 529 plans for his children.

A few weeks before his 46th birthday, tragedy strikes. While at work, Steve suffers a major heart attack and passes away that evening in the local hospital. Steve's co-workers and family are devastated while wondering how a man like Steve could suddenly be gone; especially since he was in fantastic shape due to his rigorous exercise routine and healthy eating habits.

A few weeks after the funeral, Steve's wife begins to think about how she is going to pay the mortgage, fund her children's' education plans, and retire at a reasonable age. She realizes she will have to find a job, but understands she will not make nearly as much as her husband made over the years. Steve did have a small life insurance policy through his employer that will certainly help to some extent, but it is not enough to fully protect his family's assets. Unfortunately for Steve's family, he decided that he did not need to purchase additional life insurance because he assumed nothing tragic would ever happen to him.

Amanda is a single mother of two and works hard as a restaurant manager to provide a comfortable and stable environment for her children. Although she works many hours, she always finds quality time to spend with her family and has dedicated her life to making sure her kids grow up to be responsible adults.

Amanda has also followed much of the information she learned from 'The Family Investor' and has even taught her two children about the concept of early investing. She bought them each a copy of 'The Early Investor' which they read in just under a week. Since then, they have opened up investment accounts and purchased high-quality, dividend-paying stocks, as well as low-cost index funds. (*That's called good parenting!!*)

One late summer evening, while driving home, Amanda suddenly veers out of control to avoid a family of deer attempting to cross the road. Her car slams forcefully into a tree. She miraculously survives the crash, but becomes mentally disabled and will need to have someone take care of her the rest of her life. Disability benefits *might* be approved by the government, but it will not be enough to replace her income from her job that she can no longer perform. Her family is now in danger of losing what they have accumulated over the years.

The Sullivans live in a quiet community in a suburb near a major city. The children enjoy playing with the other kids on the block and the families have many social gatherings during the year. In the cooler months, much of their free time is spent indoors, enjoying the amazing movie room they built and entertaining friends and family in the bar room.

One night, while they were asleep, the Sullivans awoke to a screeching fire alarm and quickly realized their rooms were filling up with smoke. Fortunately, they all escaped safely to the outside. Horrified, they looked on as firefighters tried to extinguish the flames of the home they loved so much.

Because the Sullivans had sufficient homeowner's insurance, their home (also known as their *dwelling*) was fully replaceable and was rebuilt over the next year. However, in addition to lost photographs and other sentimental items, the Sullivans were not able to have their home furnishings replaced by the insurance company. Their awesome movie room and bar room accessories, other furniture, and all the interior items of the house will have to be paid for by the Sullivans. Unfortunately, they did not understand that their homeowner's policy did not provide replacement cost for their interior belongings. Their policy simply covered the replacement of their dwelling.

Matthew is an intelligent young adult who has had a successful early career. He has embraced the information he read from 'The Early Investor' when he was a teenager and, consequently, has already built up a sizable investment portfolio. Matthew also lives a modestly frugal life, but still has money set aside to enjoy himself. He is well on his way to becoming independently wealthy.

Last year, Matthew bought a three-year old car that was in great shape and very reliable. His car is nothing fancy, but only has 30,000 miles on it. He made a small down payment when he purchased it and financed the rest over four years. He easily makes the car payments due to his budget and the fact that he has learned to be financially responsible.

About ten months after buying the car, Matthew was involved in a terrible accident that totaled his car. Matthew walked away without major injuries, but realized the accident was his fault. Unfortunately for Matthew, he did not purchase collision insurance as part of his auto insurance policy and will have to continue to make payments for the next few years on a car he can no longer drive.

The short stories above are not intended to scare you or cause unnecessary grief, but to make you aware of unfortunate events that can happen in your life. More specifically, unfortunate events that may cause your entire financial plan and goals to disintegrate in a matter of days or even hours. Maybe you know someone in your family who has lived through one of these scenarios or something similar to one of them. Aside from the mourning and emotional stress that these events cause, there is a harsh financial reality that we must face when the dust settles. Insurance helps manage the risks associated with your financial goals and helps protect your wealth, and more importantly, your family.

In this *exciting* chapter (more sarcasm) highlighting insurance needs, you will learn about wealth protection and how to manage different types of risk. Quite frankly, this is probably the most difficult topic I teach in my Wealth Management classes due to its gloomy nature. Furthermore, it is one of the most misunderstood and confusing subjects among many adults.

I fully understand that many people think that some forms of insurance are unnecessary and that insurance companies are not here to actually help us. For the most part, I tend to agree. Insurance companies are much like other financial institutions. They are not our friends. They are for-profit businesses formed for one sole purpose--to make money! They even have people working for them (called Actuaries) that calculate the minimum amount an insurance company can charge, yet still make the maximum possible profit. I understand *that* part of it as well because they are in the business of making money. They need to be paid for their products and services. However, please keep in mind that many of these companies will try to find *any* reason NOT to pay out insurance benefits. As an accumulator of wealth, you need to be vigilant in what an insurance policy covers. Know the specifics. Ask questions if you are unsure. Clarify. Accept the responsibility of making sure your insurance policy protects exactly what you need protected. Moving forward, the types of insurance products we will discuss include:

- Life Insurance
- Annuities
- Disability Insurance
- Homeowner's Insurance
- Auto Insurance
- Health Insurance and Long-Term Care Insurance

LIFE INSURANCE

Life insurance is not an investment. Again, life insurance is NOT an investment. I don't care how many people try to make this outrageous claim. Please do not fall into this trap. Life insurance is simply a way to protect one's family upon the death of another family member who provides significant income to the household. Some readers may have already been approached by an insurance salesman or financial advisor about purchasing insurance as an investment. Please do not succumb to their sales tactics. They might show you fancy illustrations, a variety of complex financial tables, and other marketing gimmicks to convince you that your life insurance policy can be used as a long-term investment. And if you are a financial services professional reading this book, please know that I recognize that *most* insurance professionals and financial advisors do what is in the client's best interest. However, I become deeply frustrated when I hear that someone was sold an inappropriate life insurance policy. Sometimes a life insurance policy is sold because it generates higher commissions for the insurance salesperson. Therefore, my goal is to help you gain an understanding of the basics of life insurance, review the various types of life insurance, and recommend the best and most affordable type of life insurance for *most* people.

Before we learn about the types of life insurance available, let's talk about who actually needs it. If you are single and have no dependents, you really do not need life insurance. However, if you have anyone who is financially dependent on you, it is a very wise decision to have it. Therefore, some of the questions you should consider are as follows:

1. *Do I really need life insurance?*
2. *If so, how much will I need?*
3. *Can I purchase enough life insurance through my employer?*
4. *Should I only purchase life insurance outside of my employer?*
5. *How long of a policy will I need?*

6. *Am I healthy enough to get a decent rate for my life insurance policy?*
7. *What type of policy should I purchase?*

Your life insurance needs will depend on many factors including:

- Your personal circumstances
- Your current income and expenses
- Your current savings and investments
- Your liabilities
- Your family's financial goals
- Your family's education needs
- Your retirement plan

Generally speaking, six to ten times your gross annual income is an appropriate amount of life insurance coverage. Keep in mind that every person and every family has a unique set of circumstances that may alter the amount of life insurance needed. For example, a family who has a severely autistic child will probably need more life insurance because the child will need continual care for his or her entire life. If tragedy strikes one parent or both parents of the family, a life insurance policy should be in place to help pay for the enormous costs of ongoing care. Below is a list of the life insurance policies we will cover:

- Term Life Insurance
- Whole Life Insurance (also known as Permanent Insurance)
- Universal Life Insurance
- Variable Life Insurance
- Variable Universal Life Insurance

Term Life Insurance. Term life insurance is the most common type of life insurance for good reasons and is quite simplistic. You pay a reasonable yearly amount (known as the *premium*) and you are protected for the life of the policy. Normally, the maximum amount of years of protection is 30. However, some policies might allow you to renew your policy after the initial 30 years, albeit for a much higher premium. Think of term life insurance as a rental. When you rent something, you pay for its use, return it, and do not get your money back. With term insurance, you pay an annual premium, receive a death benefit in case of the insured's death, but do not get back the premium you already paid (unless you add a Return of Premium option). In fact, if the insured outlives the policy, the death benefit is 'given back' unless the insured decides to renew the policy. Some highlights of a term insurance policy include:

- Protects your beneficiaries against financial loss resulting from your death
- Excellent coverage for an affordable price
- Coverage is limited to a specific time period
- Does not build up a cash value like other life insurance policies

For the overwhelming majority of people, term life insurance is usually the best option to help protect your family's wealth in the case of your death. Once again, it is the most affordable type of life insurance and provides excellent coverage throughout the term of the policy.

I would like to spend a little time educating you about how a financial services professional is compensated when selling life insurance to his or her clients. Regarding term life insurance, the commissions they receive are easy to understand. For example, if a client purchases a term life insurance policy with an annual premium of $500, the financial services professional will likely be paid no more than $500 (or maybe slightly less). The important concept to remember is that he or she will only be paid *one* time and one time only. Conversely, the other types of life insurance policies we will soon discuss pays the financial services professional a much larger initial commission because the annual premium will be significantly higher. Furthermore, he or she will be paid what is called a 'trailing commission' *every* year the policy premium is paid. The annual trailing commission is certainly lower than the initial commission, but nevertheless is still money in their pockets. Do you understand now why they would rather sell you any type of life insurance policy other than a standard term policy?

Another important aspect of term life insurance is that the annual premium is consistent among insurance companies and even online websites that provide term insurance quotes. In other words, it is what it is. Many people think they can get a lower rate online for term insurance when compared to getting a quote from a professional. For example, if your financial advisor gets a quote from company XYZ offering you a $400,000, 30-year term life insurance policy for an annual premium of $500, you will NOT be able to find the same policy from company XYZ for any cheaper. It does not matter if you receive a quote from any other financial services professional or if you request a quote from an online life insurance website. Same policy, same company, equals same premium. Of course, if you get a quote for the same policy, but through a different insurance company, the premium will likely be different. That is why it is very important to receive quotes from various companies to make sure you are getting the best deal. An insurance professional who is employed by one insurance company might only be able to provide you quotes from his or her company. The smartest way to shop for life insurance is to work with a professional who can offer you term life insurance from many companies. If you would like to receive an unbiased term life insurance quote from a wide variety of companies, please email me directly at mike@vikingwm.com and I will get back to you within 48 hours.

Whole Life Insurance (or Permanent Insurance). While term life insurance provides protection for a specific time period, whole life insurance provides guaranteed insurance protection for the entire life of the insured. This type of insurance also produces a 'cash value' that accumulates interest on a tax-deferred basis. Highlights of a whole life insurance policy include:

- The premiums are usually the same (or level) for the life of the insured
- The death benefit is guaranteed for the insured's lifetime
- Part of your premium is applied toward the insurance portion of the policy
- Part of your premium goes toward administrative expenses
- The remaining part of your premium goes toward the cash portion of the policy
- The interest you accumulate through the cash portion of the policy is tax-free until you withdraw it

You may be wondering why I am not advocating whole life insurance given the seemingly incredible benefits of these types of policies. The answer is relatively simple. It is because of the much higher annual premium you will need to pay. Choosing a whole life policy can negatively affect your monthly budget and can prove to be inflexible. Yes, the insurance protection you receive will far outlast a term policy, but at that point in your life you will likely not need it. That is because you will have already paid for your children's' education expenses, paid off most or all of your mortgage, accumulated enough wealth to pass on to your heirs, and significantly reduced your monthly expenses in retirement. Why would you need it anymore? The only reason to have the protection in your elder years would be if you wanted to leave a financial legacy for your children or grandchildren. I can understand those intentions, but there can be better ways to achieve that goal.

Having a cash value portion of a life insurance policy also seems like a fantastic way to accumulate wealth. And it certainly has its advantages such as tax-deferred growth. However, if you analyze the numbers in a whole life insurance policy, you will notice that your money does not grow much at all in the early years of the policy. It is very similar to a 30-year mortgage payment where most of the payment goes towards interest in the early years of the mortgage. The reason why the cash value hardly grows in the beginning is due to the high costs associated with the policy. Additionally, you will not see significant growth in the cash value for a long, long time. There are much better alternatives to save for retirement and build wealth such as many of the investments and retirement accounts we discussed in earlier chapters.

Universal Life Insurance: The only major difference between a universal life insurance policy and a whole life policy is that the premiums, cash values, and amount of the death benefit can be adjusted up or down. This provides flexibility which is why these types of policies are also known as *flexible premium* or *adjustable life*.

Variable Life Insurance: Variable life insurance is a life insurance product that has 'sub-accounts' where the insured can invest a portion of the annual premium into mutual funds. While, at first glance, these policies seem like a great combination of insurance protection and investing, it is important to understand that the expenses of variable life policies far outweigh its advantages. Consider the fact that all mutual funds come with annual expenses represented by their expense ratios. In addition to the mutual fund expenses, there are a variety of other fees that are mysteriously found in the fine print of variable life insurance policy. Remember, life insurance is NOT an investment. Why invest in mutual funds within an insurance policy when you can invest in them within a variety of investment and retirement accounts where fees are considerably less? Furthermore, always remember how a financial services professional gets paid when selling these types of policies.

Variable Universal Life Insurance: This type of insurance policy combines the features of universal life with variable life while providing flexibility to adjust premiums, death benefits and the selection of investments. One of the main disadvantages of a variable universal life insurance policy is that all the investment risk lies with the policy owner. This may cause the value of the death benefit to increase or decrease depending on the performance of the investments. One positive regarding Variable Life and Variable Universal Life policies is that your investments grow on a tax-deferred basis, similar to 401k plans and Traditional IRAs.

(Variable life insurance is a long-term investment suitable for retirement funding and subject to market fluctuations and investment risk, including the possibility of loss of principal. They generally contain fees and charges which include, but are not limited to, mortality and expense risk charges, sales and surrender charges, administrative fees, charges for optional benefits and riders, and annual contract fees. Guarantees, including guarantees associated with benefit riders are subject to the claims-paying ability of the insurance company. Surrender charges may apply if money is withdrawn before the end of the contract. All withdrawals of tax-deferred earnings are subject to current income tax, and, if made prior to age 59½, may also be subject to a 10% federal income tax penalty. Additionally, if purchased within a qualified plan, an annuity will provide no further tax deferral features. The contract, when redeemed, may be worth more or less than the total amount invested. All other benefits are available for an additional cost. It is important to weigh the costs against the benefits when adding such options to a contract.)

ANNUITIES

An annuity is a type of investment that is designed to provide an income stream in your retirement years. The reason why I discuss annuities in this chapter is because many insurance professionals push them upon their clients. While annuities carry a minimum death benefit, they are NOT life insurance products. As you can probably tell, I am not a huge fan of annuities. The debate whether annuities are good investments has been going on for years. While they have certainly become tolerable, they are still quite expensive and are extremely difficult for the average person to comprehend. Some of the expenses include the following:

- Mortality and Expense Charges
- Surrender Charges
- Rider Charges
- Management Fees

Pension plans are just annuities in disguise. The only difference is that a pension plan is a group annuity. Ever buy a lottery ticket or know someone who won a considerable amount of money playing the lottery? Well, the money you win from the lottery is wrapped up in an annuity. Generally speaking, you put money into an annuity and allow it to grow on a tax-deferred basis (the accumulation phase). Then, at some point in retirement, you begin taking a stream of payments (the annuitization phase). You will find that some annuities are marketed as providing a guarantee. With the exception of fixed annuities, *there are no investment guarantees when purchasing an annuity*. If I decide to recommend an annuity to a client, I am unable to even use the word "guarantee" because it is very misleading. Please be careful when considering annuities. Read the fine print. Understand the terms. Ask questions. Admittingly, like any other investment, annuities *might* have a place in your investment portfolio. However, please consider all of your options before signing an annuity contract.

Fixed Annuities: A fixed annuity does have guaranteed principal and interest (as long as the insurance company remains in business!). You add money to it and you receive interest payments based on current economic conditions and current interest rates. Similar to all annuities, any earnings you generate within an annuity grow on a tax-deferred basis. You begin receiving payments at some point in the future.

Variable Annuities: Variable annuities work much like variable life insurance policies in that you can invest in mutual funds within the contract. However, the payment amount you are able to receive in the future may be determined by the performance of your investments. Therefore, the amount you receive can be dependent on market conditions and can vary widely. Some variable annuities do offer something called a '*guaranteed minimum income benefit*' or GMIB (*please be aware that insurance companies may refer to a GMIB by a different name*). The "guarantee" simply means that if the performance of the investments within the annuity do not exceed a specified guaranteed amount or rate, you can "annuitize" at the higher value. What that means is you can choose to begin taking payments at the GMIB value. For example, if the actual value of your variable annuity is $125,000 based on the performance of the underlying investments, but the GMIB annuitized value is $175,000, you can lock in the $175,000 GMIB value as long as you begin taking payments (annuitize). This sounds fantastic on the surface, but keep in mind that you never want to have to annuitize your annuity. Once you annuitize, your income from the annuity will cease to exist at some point in time. You certainly have numerous options to receive income payments, but your flexibility has significantly diminished. Unlike IRAs and other retirement accounts where your beneficiaries can inherit the accounts, annuities limit the ability to continue its benefits after annuitizing. Most variable annuities allow you to choose the GMIB after ten years. Similar to Variable Life Insurance, you are also paying expenses to the mutual fund managers as well as the typical annuity fees listed above. This can take a sizable chunk out of your long-term return.

(Annuities are long-term investments suitable for retirement funding and are subject to market fluctuations and investment risk, including the possibility of loss of principal. Annuities generally contain fees and charges which include, but are not limited to, mortality and expense risk charges, sales and surrender charges, administrative fees, charges for optional benefits and riders, and annual contract fees. Annuity guarantees, including guarantees associated with benefit riders are subject to the claims-paying ability of the insurance company. Surrender charges may apply if money is withdrawn before the end of the contract. All withdrawals of tax-deferred earnings are subject to current income tax, and, if made prior to age 59½, may also be subject to a 10% federal income tax penalty. Additionally, if purchased within a qualified plan, an annuity will provide no further tax deferral features. The contract, when redeemed, may be worth more or less than the total amount invested. All other benefits are available for an additional cost. It is important to weigh the costs against the benefits when adding such options to an annuity contract.)

Deferred Annuities: Fixed annuities and variable annuities are considered deferred annuities. Deferred annuities refer to the fact that you receive payments at a later date.

Immediate Annuities: Immediate annuities are designed for people who want to make a sizable investment and receive payments right away. Therefore, there is no accumulation phase and no underlying investments. Please be cognizant of what is called the "*annuitization rate*". The annuitization rate is the rate at which your income stream payments are calculated. Annuitization rates of annuities tend to be quite low. Therefore, other types of investments, such as bonds, may prove to more suitable for your income needs.

DISABILITY INSURANCE

The possibility of becoming at least temporarily disabled during your working career is much higher than the possibility of dying during your working career. Even so, most people will purchase life insurance and stay away from purchasing disability Insurance. That is because disability insurance tends to be significantly more expensive than life insurance. However, as part of your wealth protection plan, disability insurance can prevent financial disaster if you become disabled on a long-term basis. Many people believe that social security will provide them with sufficient disability income. That could not be farther from the truth. Quite frankly, it may be difficult to qualify for disability benefits through social security. And while some people have access to a <u>limited</u> coverage disability plan through their pension or government benefit plan, many of us do not.

Disability insurance policies offer a variety of characteristics including:

- Any Occupation
- Modified Any Occupation
- Own Occupation
- Split Definition
- Loss of Income

Any occupation is when the insured is considered disabled only if he or she is unable to perform any job tasks related to any occupation. *Modified any occupation* is when you are unable to perform any job tasks related to any occupation for which you have been trained, received education or have work experience. *Own occupation* is when you are considered disabled if you are unable to engage in the principal duties of your own occupation. *Split definition* is within one's own occupation for a specific period of time or with any occupation after the maximum benefit period has passed. *Loss of income* is when a policy pays the insured in the event of loss of income due to an illness or injury.

There are two types of duration when shopping for disability coverage:

- Short Term-This type of coverage provides coverage for disabilities of up to two years, but most policies pay up to six months on average.
- Long Term-This type of coverage protects for a longer time period, often until age 65 or for life.

The premiums that insurance companies charge for a disability policy are based on the amount of risk involved in your job. Furthermore, some jobs will not even allow you to qualify for disability insurance, For example, if you wash windows on skyscrapers, it is unlikely that any insurance company will provide coverage.

There are many other factors to consider when purchasing disability coverage such as:

- Elimination Periods
- Probation Period
- Disability Insurance Riders

The elimination period is the amount of time you have to wait before benefits are paid after you become disabled. Basically, the longer the elimination period, the lower your premium. Typical elimination periods can be anywhere between 30 and 90 days. In some cases, they can be even longer. Disability payments usually do not begin until 30 days after the elimination period ends. (Wouldn't you like to be an insurance company?!)

The probation period is the amount of time a policy must be in force before it covers the insured for undisclosed pre-existing conditions. This obviously protects the insurance company in the event the insured is recovering from a medical condition.

There are many disability insurance riders to choose from for an additional premium. Two of the most common are *guaranteed insurability* and *cost of living adjustments* (COLA). Guaranteed insurability gives you the ability to purchase additional insurance with no further health evaluation. COLA increases your benefits by an amount equal to the increase in the consumer price index; a measure of inflation. I firmly believe that the COLA rider is necessary for proper wealth protection.

HOMEOWNER'S INSURANCE

If you own a home, and have a mortgage, you are required to have homeowner's insurance. Homeowner's insurance is broken into four categories:

1. Dwelling
2. Other Structures
3. Personal Property
4. Loss of Use

The *dwelling* is simply the structure on the property (your physical home). *Other structures* refers to structures that are not part of the house such as a shed or detached garage. *Personal property* refers to the contents in your home such as furniture and appliances. Keep in mind, personal property may not cover items like jewelry. That is why one of the most important additions to add to your homeowner's policy is *replacement cost*. While some policies provide replacement cost as part of their basic policy, many do not. Replacement cost is when the insurance company allows you to be reimbursed for the purchase of a similar item that has been damaged, destroyed, or stolen. Furthermore, be careful the insurance company doesn't just cover the *actual cash value* of an item. The actual cash value option will only reimburse you the current value of a damaged, destroyed, or stolen item. For example, let's say that you have a TV that needs to be replaced. If you only had actual cash value coverage on your policy and the TV was four years old, you would only be reimbursed for the current value at the time (obviously less than what you paid for it). With replacement cost coverage, the insurance company will allow you to buy a brand new similar television and reimburse the full cost to you. Finally, *loss of use* will provide the reimbursement of any cost of living expenses if your home becomes uninhabitable.

Other types of homeowner's insurance coverage you need to be aware of include:

- Fire
- Tornadoes
- Floods
- Earthquakes
- Wildfires
- Hail

Most policies will not cover earthquakes and floods, but most will cover you against hurricanes, tornadoes, and hail storms. As of this writing, almost all (if not all) policies will cover you against wildfires.

When selecting homeowner's insurance, you need to choose an appropriate *deductible*. A deductible is the amount of money you will need to pay the insurance company before they reimburse you or pay a claim. For example, let's say a large tree falls in your backyard and damages your fence. The estimated cost to remove the tree and replace the broken part of the fence is $2,500. If your deductible is $1,000, then the insurance company will only pay $1,500 since you are responsible to pay the first $1,000. Generally, the higher the deductible, the lower your annual premium. Conversely, the lower the deductible, the higher the annual premium.

AUTO INSURANCE

Auto insurance is another type of wealth protection that is mandatory for drivers in almost all of the 50 states. Auto insurance falls into five major categories:

1. Liability
2. Collision
3. Personal Injury Protection
4. Uninsured Motorist
5. Comprehensive

Liability insurance is the minimum auto insurance coverage required in most states. This type of insurance will protect you against injury or death to other drivers involved in an accident that was caused by you or anyone on the policy. This type of coverage will not cover against injuries to you or anyone else on the policy. Standard liability insurance will cover medical, pain and suffering, funeral, loss of income, and legal expenses up to policy limits. I recommend that you obtain liability insurance that covers a minimum of up to $100,000 per person and $300,000 per accident.

Collision insurance will replace any vehicle covered that has been deemed 'totaled' or heavily damaged in an accident. Collision insurance is not mandatory by the state you live in. However, if you have a loan out on the car, most lenders will require that you have collision insurance. That is rightfully so because if you total your car and do not have collision insurance, you have no car and will still have to make the monthly car payments. That is definitely not a good wealth protection strategy. The deductible you choose for collision insurance should be between $250 and $1,000. Some lenders require a minimum deductible as well.

Personal injury protection is not mandatory in all states. However, this is still important to obtain because it provides coverage for bodily injury to you or anyone on the policy. Your health care may also provide coverage against bodily injury, but it is a good idea to have personal injury protection just in case.

Uninsured motorist bodily injury coverage pays for medical bills for you and any passengers if you are hit by a driver who is uninsured. Sometimes the other driver has insurance, but it is not sufficient to cover all of the expense. In this case, *underinsured motorist bodily injury* will pay the difference between his or her policy limits and yours.

Comprehensive insurance covers against vehicle damage other than collision including:

- Broken windshield
- Fire

- Theft
- Vandalism
- Damage from floods, hurricanes, tornadoes, wind, objects, or animals

Similar to collision insurance, comprehensive insurance is not mandatory, but could be required by your lender. The deductible you choose for comprehensive insurance should be between $250 and $1,000 as well.

Some states, including my home state of Pennsylvania, let the insured choose between the *full tort* and *limited tort* option. When selecting the full tort option, the insured has the full right to sue a negligent party, including non-monetary damages. When selecting the limited tort option, the insured can only sue for the amount of the medical expenses incurred and the expenses related to any car damage. Limited tort is certainly cheaper, but full tort gives you better options to recuperate your wealth in the event of serious harm caused by another driver.

HEALTH INSURANCE

Health insurance is an extremely important type of insurance because it covers the cost of most medical expenses. Without it, a severe illness or accident can cause financial disaster for you and your family. Most people purchase health insurance through their employer at a discount, but some people, including many self-employed individuals, need to purchase insurance on their own. The types of coverage for expenses varies depending on the type of plan. The types of health insurance plans available include, but are not limited to, the following:

- Health Maintenance Organization (HMO)
- Preferred Provider Organization (PPO)
- Indemnity Plan
- Point of Service (POS)

The HMO is probably the most common type of insurance policy people purchase and the one most frequently provided by employers. One of the reasons why they are popular is because the premiums are usually lower than most other plans. With HMOs, you must choose a primary care physician (or PCP) who oversees your health. If you need to see a specialist, you must first obtain a referral from your PCP. In the past, getting a referral proved to be quite tedious and aggravating. However, with the technology revolution in the medical industry, referrals are now done electronically. Therefore, your PCP will automatically and instantly send the referral to the specialist you wish to see. Generally speaking, if you and your family are in good health, an HMO makes the most sense.

One negative about HMOs is that you can only select doctors and hospitals approved in the insurance carrier's network. However, most doctors and hospitals in your local area will be part of the network. It is important that you make sure your current doctor is in the network if you wish to keep him or her.

Preferred Provider Organizations (or PPOs) are a group of health care providers that contract with insurance companies, third-party administrators, and employers. They provide medical services at a reasonable cost. PPOs differ from HMOs in a couple of ways:

- The providers in the PPO are paid on a fee-for-service basis as needed

- With PPOs, you can visit doctors outside of the network, but that usually results in higher costs and/or higher copayments and deductibles

An Indemnity Plan is sometimes referred to as a fee-for-service plan. This plan reimburses you according to a schedule for medical expenses, regardless of who provides the service. With indemnity plans, the insurer will pay a specified amount per day for a limited number of days. These plans cover things such as:

- Hospital stays
- Surgical expenses
- Major medical coverage

A Point of Service Plan (or POS) is a combination of the health insurance plans above. This type of plan is more flexible in that it allows you to decide at the time you need services to elect to use in-network care or to go outside the network or hospital and pay a higher portion of the cost.

LONG-TERM CARE INSURANCE

You have a much greater chance in your lifetime becoming disabled during your working years than spending significant time in a nursing home after you retire. However, the financial reality of nursing home and assisted living costs should cause you to explore long-term care insurance. These costs have risen dramatically over the years and *could* wipe out much of a person's wealth. While Medicaid will provide payment for these costs, the United States has changed many of the laws for Medicaid eligibility, essentially making it extremely difficult to receive it unless your assets have been drawn down to a minimum. Keep in mind that the "sweet spot" for purchasing long-term care insurance is usually between 55 and 60 years of age. You will find that this type of insurance can be very expensive, but could prevent you from depleting most of your accumulated wealth.

Within a long-term care policy there are usually three levels of care outlined in the policy, including:

1. **Skilled Nursing Care**: This is for people with a sudden and severe condition that requires intensive medical attention for a period of less than 100 days. The two objectives of skilled care are to help the person with comfort and assistance if the situation is terminal or to assist the person during recovery.
2. **Hospice Care**: This is the term used for the care provided to individuals facing a terminal condition, or who have less than six months to live. This care can be provided in a home or a facility.
3. **Non-Skilled Nursing Care/Custodial Care**: This is for a person with a chronic condition from which he or she will not recover. This type of care is usually received at home or in assisted living facilities. This type of care usually lasts more than 100 days.

While it is ultimately up to you whether or not you want to purchase long-term care insurance at some point in your life, please understand the possible financial ramifications if you or your loved ones are caught without it. Additionally, most people wait until it is too late to be approved for long-term care insurance. For example, if you are diagnosed with Alzheimer's disease or another sickness that requires the services mentioned above, you will be unable to find any insurance company that will approve you for this type of coverage. At that point, you will be expected to deplete your assets until they reach the minimum amount allowed to be Medicaid eligible. Visit medicaid.gov to read about the current eligibility requirements for Medicaid.

<u>Key Points to Remember from Chapter 8</u>

- Term insurance is the most cost efficient way to protect your family
- Understand the terms of an annuity and realize they can be very expensive
- Disability insurance can be costly, but many of us will be disabled during our working years
- Make sure you understand your homeowner's policy and that it includes replacement cost
- If you have a loan out on your car, you need collision insurance
- Choose a health care plan that fits your family's needs
- Consider long-term care insurance at some point in your life to protect your accumulated wealth

CHAPTER NINE

—◆—

IDENTITY THEFT, FINANCIAL FRAUD, AND THE RISKS OF SOCIAL MEDIA

Victor Victim received a check from an unfamiliar business made out to him for $5,000 that was sent through a reputable delivery service. He was certainly skeptical about the validity of the check. Victor then received a phone call soon after from someone who claimed they were an account manager from the business who sent the check. The account manager apologized for the misunderstanding and politely told Victor that he could keep $1,000 for the inconvenience it caused him. However, Victor was told he had to wire the other $4,000 back to the business right away. Victor decided to take "advantage" of the nice offer from the account manager and followed the instructions to wire the account manager $4,000. A few days later the $5,000 check he deposited bounced, triggering fees from his bank. Victor was defrauded out of $4,000 plus the bank fees. Victor was a victim of fake check fraud.

Grandma Gullible receives an urgent phone call from someone claiming to be her granddaughter. The granddaughter makes an emotional plea for Grandma Gullible to wire $3,000 to Canada to bail her out of jail. The tearful granddaughter also begs Grandma not to tell her mother what has happened. It appears that her granddaughter was supposed to be away with her friend's family, but decided to take a road trip into Canada with her new boyfriend as well as some illegal substances that were discovered by the police. Making the phone call seem even more real, the 'police captain' gets on the phone and convincingly provides details of the events to Grandma Gullible. Grandma feels terrible for her granddaughter and senses the urgency of the situation. She proceeds to drive to the nearest Western Union and wires the money with the account information that was provided. Just a few hours later, Grandma Gullible decides to call her son and daughter-in-law because she knows it is the right thing to do. Much to her surprise, her son tells her that her granddaughter is sitting right next to him at home. Grandma Gullible is a victim of the grandparent scam.

Nathan Naive answers the phone and listens in horror as the pre-recorded call from the Internal Revenue Service instructs him to send $1,500 right away due to overdue taxes that he apparently never paid. Furthermore, he is warned that if the IRS does not receive the payment within the next few hours, a warrant will be issued for his immediate arrest. Now in full panic mode, Nick follows the instructions and uses a pre-paid debit card to pay the money he supposedly owes. Nathan is a victim of the IRS phone call scam.

The number of scams and types of fraud are seemingly endless in today's world. Here are a few extraordinary statistics:

- There have been over 800 million personal records exposed from 2005 to 2015 alone.[1]
- $16 billion stolen from 12.7 million identity fraud victims in 2014.[2]

---

[1] Statistics provided by the Identity Theft Resource Center, idtheftcenter.org, 2016

- 17.6 million U.S. residents experienced some form of identity theft in 2014.[3]

Examples of common scams include charity scams, IRS related scams, phishing, free computer security scams, chain letters, phantom debt scams, pyramid schemes, fake check scams, and international financial scams. Common types of fraud include virtually every type of industry including banking, healthcare, mail fraud, telemarketing, and much more. No one is immune. Furthermore, the people who attempt to defraud honest citizens are not biased in who they choose to scam. Retirees, teenagers, celebrities, newborns (yes, children as young as infants have also been affected), mothers, fathers, and many businesses are all targets for scam artists. Again, no one is immune!

In this final chapter, my goal is to inform and educate you on the risks of financial fraud and identity theft. Think of identity theft as making a copy of yourself and having someone use that information to conduct fraud under your name. Furthermore, *you* will be responsible for all of the consequences. Although identity theft may not occur as often as other types of fraud, one of the main issues is the length of time it takes (potentially years) to rectify the situation. Some of the ramifications of identity theft include:

- Ruining your credit rating
- Difficulty in obtaining loans and lines of credit
- Credit cards taken out under your name
- Life insurance policies taken out under your name
- Difficulty in signing up for a cell phone plan
- Potential problems in buying a home

---

[2] 2015 Identity Fraud Study by Javelin Strategy & Research, March 2015
[3] Victims of Identity Theft, 2014, 2014 Identity Theft Supplement to the National Crime Victimization Survey, September 2015

- Possible issues with being hired for a job

I believe this chapter is extremely important in maintaining your financial integrity and in reducing your family's susceptibility to scam artists. Remember, it only takes *one* time for your personal information to be compromised and to have your identity and accumulated wealth stolen. Additionally, we will also discuss how social media can potentially be harmful to your career and your personal well-being.

Rather than write about these topics using only my personal knowledge, I took the time to interview various professionals in fraud awareness and prevention. While I certainly am educated about the numerous scams and illegal activities that are part of everyday life now, I was shocked at the scope of the problem. I was also amazed at the clever ways in which people can be defrauded. Some of the questions I asked the panel of experts included:

- Can you speak to the reality of identity theft and fraud and how it has significantly affected our society?
- What are some of the greatest risks to a family regarding financial fraud?
- How can/does financial fraud completely change a family's financial goals and/or accumulated wealth?
- Regarding financial fraud, how would you tell young couples/families to protect themselves from scams/social media/etc.?
- Where can a family turn to if they have become victims of scam artists/identity theft?
- How can people rectify their situation if they are a victim of identity theft?
- What would you tell young couples and families about the dangers/risks of social media?

The first person I interviewed was Robert Siciliano, the CEO of IDTheftSecurity.com. Robert is a well-known author of numerous books on identity theft including '*99 Things You Wish You Knew Before Your Identity Was Stolen*'. He is also on the Board of Directors of The Identity Theft Resource Center, a service that provides free education and assistance in identity theft prevention. Here are a few of Robert's thoughts and suggestions:

"The fact is, to this very day, human beings globally have not been effectively identified. This means we use paper and plastic in American identifiers that are inconsistent with the actual human. At any point these documents or identifiers can be applied to another human. Until this problem is fixed there will be a significant lack of accountability, resulting in fraud. With new account fraud, new lines of credit can be opened which generally means the thief will not pay the bill, resulting in bad credit. Account takeover fraud means existing accounts are drained or fraudulent transactions are created often resulting in lost time and money. Depending on the severity of the fraud, it certainly could change a family's goals or accumulated wealth. However, as long as someone is paying relatively close attention to account activities they should be able to refute fraud and make themselves whole. Become familiar with all the various scams so you know what to look for. Don't post every last detail about your lives that could allow a criminal the ability to reset account passwords by using the 'forgot password' feature based on knowledge-based authentication questions found in social media. If you become a victim of identity theft or financial fraud, the proper response for resolution depends on the nature of the theft. Generally, victims should freeze their credit. Additionally, file a police report. Then contact every lender or creditor who was affected and go through their individual processes for restoration.

Regarding social media, both young and old are in the same situation of posting just way too much revealing information in regards to their personal and professional lives that would allow criminals to socially engineer or call on them via phone or email in a number of ways.

Consumers should seriously consider investing in identity theft protection products. Between identity theft protection and a credit freeze, consumers should be tight in regards to preventing new account fraud. Otherwise, they need to pay close attention to all of their lines of credit and seek out unauthorized activity on a daily basis."

Steve Purdy, Vice President of Sales & Marketing for a global leader in digital identification solutions, has been involved in government security programs for over 20 years. Steve provides an interesting background on how the United States handles identity theft and fraud protection:

In short, identity theft and financial fraud are huge and rampant problems. The large financial institutions have been working on creating a more secure environment, using smart card technology, to handle financial transactions. EMV (Europay, MasterCard, Visa) created a standard to be used across all banks and countries, but the United States was very slow in adopting smart card technology", Steve says. *"We are now seeing that technology spreading across the country. Banks are issuing new cards with chips on it with many retailers getting new payment terminals to accept these chips."*

When the general public hears "smart card technology", they typically associate two different chip technologies:

1. **RFID (Radio Frequency Identification)**-Most people associate their passport, EMV cards, and other personal

identity documents with RFID, but that is very misleading. RFID has *minimal* security, but does offer maximum convenience. Normally, this technology contains a unique identifier, but offers little or no protection to read it. When read, it pulls up an account number or id number that allows an agency or business to pull up pertinent information about you from their database.

2. **Smart Card Technology**-This technology utilizes microprocessor chips which provide secure containers for personal information. EMV cards, for example, use this smart card technology. Smart card technology also encrypts data that was exchanged and requires two-factor authentication. Two-factor authentication may include a pin number, a passport machine readable zone (MRZ), or even biometric fingerprints. At all times you are giving authorization to allow someone to access your information.

Many people feel that smart card technology is intrusive and invades people's privacy which can be used to track what they are doing. The reality is that it is not a device that can be used to track. It is a passive device. Most of us use smartphones that can be tracked, but we do not seem to mind. For example, we ask Google to tell us where specific locations are and we have tracking apps that can tell us where our children are located.

Steve offers some great advice on how to protect yourself against identity theft and fraud:

- Limit online shopping to trusted sites with web pages beginning with **https** (the "s" stands for secure).
- Limit personal and financial information in emails. One must assume that this information is completely exposed when sending.

- Try not to use debit cards for shopping. If somebody gets access to your debit card information, they are gaining access to your checking account which is not protected by Visa/MasterCard.
- If you get a letter from a company saying that their database was hacked and your credit card info might be compromised, change your credit card right away.
- Use long, complex passwords including alphanumeric and symbols.
- Do not use the same password for every account.
- The more damage a compromise can cause, the more sophisticated the password should be.
- Never trust any person online. The fact that hackers can get personal information from businesses does not bode well for your personal well-being on social media.

Steve, along with many of us, gets at least 2-3 emails a day asking him for investment funds. Some of the emails claim they need a bank to deposit a large sum of money and that they will let him keep a percentage of it. He also receives emails from phony financial websites saying that there was fraudulent activity on his account and asking him to '**Click Here**' to validate his account. He says that the link will take you to a fraudulent site which looks like his bank's website. They want you to enter your account information which they proceed to steal. Steve says that banks will never call or email you to validate your account information. Do not click or respond to any email asking for personal information. Always call the bank or other institution directly.

Stephen Harbeck is the President and CEO of the Securities Investor Protection Corporation (SIPC). The SIPC is a non-profit corporation that oversees the liquidation of member broker-dealers that close when the broker-dealer is bankrupt or in financial trouble, and customer assets are missing. SIPC protects the securities and cash in your brokerage account up to $500,000 *only* if your brokerage firm fails and it is a SIPC member. The $500,000 protection includes up to $250,000 protection for cash in your account to buy securities. Most U.S. brokerage firms are required to be SIPC members. To find out if your brokerage firm is a SIPC member, you can check the list or contact them at www.sipc.org.

Stephen says that most financial fraud at investment firms are done by someone who knows the victim. Many times it is a family member who may have access to the account or has seen the account password written on a piece of paper near a computer. Relatives can also intercept checks that were sent from the firm to the victim's address. If financial fraud by a family member does occur, it is common for the victim to sign over all criminal and/or civil rights to the investment firm because the firm will replace the assets within the account. Unfortunately, most of the complaints wind up going away because most people do not want a family member prosecuted.

According to Stephen, much of the fraud that occurs at the local level is from *affinity fraud*. Affinity fraud refers to investment scams that prey upon members of identifiable groups, such as religious or ethnic communities, the elderly, or professional groups. Members of the group have something in common so they tend to trust each other and will decide to conduct business within the group. Many times the fraudster will join a group just for this reason. They will be patient and wait for the right time to scam someone out of their money. Stephen suggests always checking someone's professional license to see if that person has had complaints filed against them in the past. Never do business with anyone without researching their background first!

If you become a victim of financial fraud, Stephen recommends going to the North American Securities Administrators Association website at www.nasaa.org. Victims can contact their state regulator from the website and file a complaint. The NASAA website also provides excellent resources to educate people on common scams and how to protect yourself.

Sharing a wealth of information and tips is Carrie Kerskie, author, speaker, and fraud and identity theft expert. Carrie is the author of '*Your Public Identity: Because Nothing is Private Anymore*' and is a private investigator herself. Her website, carriekerskie.com, provides numerous types of identity theft services for individuals and businesses. She believes that identity theft and/or financial fraud cannot be completely prevented and that you *will* become a victim at some point in your life. That is certainly a sobering thought! Carrie points out that there are many organizations that store our personal data including banks, hospitals, schools, local, state, and federal government entities, and online retailers. Even some organized sports that your children play require that you provide a copy of your child's birth certificate! Therefore, it is almost impossible to prevent yourself from becoming a victim.

If you have become a victim of fraud, Carrie says you need to report it *immediately* to law enforcement. She also recommends putting a *credit freeze* on your credit reports. A credit freeze lets you restrict access to your credit reports, which makes it more difficult for identity thieves to open new accounts under your name.

If you are a victim of identity theft, you need to contact the organization immediately to report the discrepancy. At this point you should complete and sign an *Identity Theft Victim's Complaint and Affidavit* form found at the consumer.ftc.gov website. Often organizations will ask for an "identity theft report" to be sent to them with their required forms to document the fraud. The "identity theft report" consists of the FTC affidavit and a police report. These can then be faxed or mailed **Certified Return Receipt Requested** to any bank or institution where you do business or hold a debit/credit card. Federal law will not protect you unless they receive written notification within 30 days of the fraudulent transaction. Furthermore, the reason why you mail the form with "certified return receipt requested" is so that your complaint is allowed in court, if necessary. Companies, including banks, will not give you this pertinent information because they do not want to be responsible for a fraudulent incident stemming from identity theft.

Although it is difficult to prevent identity theft and fraud completely, Carrie has some useful recommendations to help reduce your risk:

- Do not wait for monthly financial statements. Monitor your accounts online every few days.
- Set up an online presence to prevent scammers from setting up online accounts if they have your personal information.
- Do not display personal information on social media websites.
- Consider placing a credit freeze on your credit report, including your children if your state allows it, to prevent new account fraud. Make sure you place the credit freeze with all three credit bureaus (Equifax/Experian/TransUnion).
- Have conversations with family members, including grandparents, about specific scams that are out there.
- Create a secret word in case you receive a call from a potential scammer claiming that he/she is a family relative.
- If you do not recognize a number on Caller Id, let it go to voicemail.
- Be aware of unsolicited phone calls or emails from scammers that usually project a sense of urgency.

- Be suspicious of any unsolicited mail, especially from FedEx or UPS because fraudsters cannot be charged with mail fraud if they get caught while using these services.

Keep in mind that setting up an online presence includes having a Facebook profile, a social security profile, and other online profiles from familiar websites. Having a Facebook account does not mean that you have to use it. It simply means that a scammer will find it difficult to open a Facebook profile under your name if it is already out there. Regarding social security, Carrie suggests establishing an online profile at www.ssa.gov to prevent scammers from defrauding you out of disability benefits and/or retirement benefits. This may sound exaggerated, but there have been many, many cases of financial fraud involving social security. Imagine applying for retirement benefits only to find out that someone has been receiving them already for years! Regarding a credit freeze, make sure you temporarily unfreeze your credit reports before applying for loans or applying for anything that requires a credit score.

David Shallcross is an Education Outreach Specialist and the Elder Abuse Unit Leader for the Pennsylvania Office of the Attorney General. He previously worked on projects for the U.S. Department of Homeland Security. David's professional experience includes 21 years working for the Bucks County, PA Sheriff's Office. He frequently speaks about identity theft and financial fraud to various age groups in the community. According to David, there are hundreds, if not thousands, of scams out there today and new ones arising every day. The following is a brief list of scams we discussed:

- Employees using personal information to commit identity theft from job applicants who were not hired

- Phone calls from scammers claiming they are from debt collection agencies
- Receiving a phone call showing the Caller ID information from a familiar business, only to discover that the person on the other line was a scam artist and the Caller ID information was generated from a phone app (this is called *spoofing*)
- "Work from home jobs" that require you to wire money to unfamiliar places or businesses

David also warns that if the Internet ever failed nationwide, it could result in crippling consequences, including turning our financial world on its side. This is because our personal information is stored digitally in a seemingly infinite number of places. A nationwide Internet failure could make that information much more vulnerable to hackers.

David is yet another expert that suggests that it is not a matter of *if* you will ever become a victim, but *when*. However, he does offer some good habits to follow to help protect yourself:

- Use contact information from trusted sources only, such as the phone number on the back of your credit card or on your bank statement
- Never trust the person on the phone who made the initial contact
- Remember that any personal business from institutions you have a relationship with will only be done through written correspondence and received through the U.S. Postal Service
- When online, do not click on any pop-ups or even the "No" or "Close" buttons on the pop-ups because they may be loaded with malware or spyware...use a Task Manager to close them

- Always check that your Internet privacy settings are set correctly and change passwords often
- Set up text and email alerts on your accounts so that you are notified of any account activity or any changes in authorized users and/or passwords
- Pay as many bills online as possible because many identity thieves will steal your personal information by noticing the raised flag on your mailbox and opening your bill payments you placed inside
- Pay cash when dining out or pay with a credit card at the register only to avoid it being out of sight
- When hiring identity theft services, do your homework by comparing prices relevant to the services and by reading the fine print
- Always look for discrepancies in your credit report
- When providing answers to security questions, never use your mother's maiden name because it can easily be found on numerous genealogy websites

USING SOCIAL MEDIA RESPONSIBLY

Let's face it! We live in a globally connected, 24/7 world with all of the incredible technology available to us right at our fingertips. At the center of this technology is a variety of social media outlets and platforms that seem to expand every day. While social media has opened the doors of communication and transformed the way we interact, establish networks, and even do our jobs, there are many substantial dangers involved when being constantly connected through our devices. Colleges, corporations, and law enforcement are all examples of institutions that can search the vast web of personal information on each one of us that is floating around in cyberspace, waiting to be discovered. Many college admissions offices will look at social media profiles of applicants to see if there are any red flags that would hinder his or her potential acceptance. Most human resources departments of corporations will search the Internet for possible red flags of job applicants. There have been many employees who have been fired from their jobs for posting inappropriate comments or pictures through social media. These are some of the reasons it is essential to understand how to use social media in a positive manner so that your quest for wealth and financial independence is not jeopardized.

Christy Sweeney is an Advisory Talent Leader for PricewaterhouseCoopers (PwC), a global leader in accounting and consulting services. Christy believes that social media can be a powerful tool which can help create a <u>positive</u> *personal brand* for yourself. She says to think of your personal brand as your reputation. There are many advantages to personal branding through social media including:

- Networking opportunities
- Promoting and marketing yourself
- Rewarding partnerships
- Leadership opportunities
- Association with people with common interests
- Greater credibility and recognition
- An influential way to discuss your area(s) of expertise

While many companies have discouraged the use of social media in the past, it is now embraced and used as an important communication and advertising tool. However, like anything else, there are always individual risks involved. Christy points out some of these risks when using social media that can have a negative effect on your career:

- Posting anything that negatively affects your personal brand
- Posting harsh political views
- Posting pictures showing you "partying" or displaying inappropriate behavior
- Posting anything private or derogatory about other people (also known as "cyberbullying")
- Posting anything on your personal social media sites during work hours
- Posting strong, negative personal views in private chat rooms or blogs

According to Christy, many recruiters use the Internet to search social media sites in order to learn more about job candidates. That is why it is so important to make sure you are branding yourself professionally. Branding yourself professionally includes creating an appropriate email address. How many times have you seen a "funny" email address from a friend or relative? You should keep your email address professional and remember that people formulate opinions of you by the way you present yourself through *all* communication channels. Additionally, anything you post through social media should be well written. Always avoid using slang and inappropriate language. Remember, in today's world, anything you put out there through cyberspace *never* goes away!

Identity theft, financial fraud, and social media are just a portion of your overall financial plan. Budgeting, establishing an emergency fund, staying out of debt, buying a home, choosing a mortgage, education planning, investment management, and wealth protection should all be important pieces of your financial puzzle. Understanding these concepts will help you become financially responsible and savvy which can lead to greater wealth and a life that is free from financial stress. I hope you enjoyed The Family Investor and I encourage you to discuss what you have learned with your family and friends. Together, we can make a significant difference in the lives of others!

Key Points to Remember from Chapter 9

- Identity theft and financial fraud are very real and global problems that can compromise your personal and financial well being
- Consider freezing your credit scores until needed
- Understand that nothing is 100% private on the Internet and social media sites
- If your identity is compromised or you become a victim of financial fraud, take the appropriate steps to protect yourself from further harm and to rectify the situation as soon as possible
- Set up an online presence so it is difficult for scammers to open new accounts under your name
- Social media can be a great tool for personal branding
- Be cognizant of anything you post on the Internet and/or social media platforms
- Never post on social media that you are going on vacation

ABOUT THE AUTHOR

Michael Zisa received his Master's degree in Mathematics Education and earned his Bachelor's degree in Business Management. After 5 ½ years as a high school Mathematics teacher in New York City, Mike had a rewarding career as a Senior Financial Analyst at Bank of America. He was also a Financial Advisor for four years in Princeton, NJ before becoming an Independent Financial Advisor. Mike has been teaching Investment Management and Wealth Management classes at Pennsbury High School in Bucks County, PA since 2004, teaches Personal Financial Planning and Business Communications classes at a local college, and has developed numerous financial literacy curriculums. Additionally, he is a Certified Financial Education Instructor through the National

Financial Educators Council (NFEC), a member of the Personal Finance Speakers Association (PFSA), and the Global Association of Teachers of Economics (GATE). Mike has written financial literacy articles for various publications, been interviewed by Forbes and U.S. News & World Report, and has been a keynote financial literacy speaker at numerous conventions. His hobbies include playing the guitar, exercising, traveling, and spending time with family and friends.

Investing in securities involves risk of loss that clients should be prepared to bear. No investment process is free of risk; no strategy or risk management technique can guarantee returns or eliminate risk in any market environment. There is no guarantee that your investment will be profitable. **Past performance is not a guide to future performance.** *The value of investments, as well any investment income, is not guaranteed and can fluctuate based on market conditions. Hypothetical examples provided are used to demonstrate mathematical principles. They do not illustrate any investment products and do not show past or future performance of any specific investment.*